A Practical Guide to
Integrated Marketing Communications

Tom Brannan

Series Editor: Norman Hart

KOGAN
PAGE

YOURS TO HAVE AND TO HOLD

BUT NOT TO COPY

First published in 1995
Revised edition 1998

Kogan Page Limited
120 Pentonville Road
London N1 9JN

British Library Cataloguing in Publication Data

A CIP record for this book is available from the British Library.

ISBN 0 7494 1520 7

Typeset by JS Typesetting, Wellingborough, Northants.
Printed in Great Britain by Biddles Ltd, Guildford and King's Lynn.

A Practical Guide to
Integrated Marketing Communications

Marketing in Action Series

Series Editor: Norman Hart

In producing this series, the advice and assistance has been sought of a prestigious editorial panel representing the principal professional bodies, trade associations and business schools.

The Series Editor for the Marketing in Action books is Norman Hart who is a writer of some ten books himself. He currently runs his own marketing consultancy, and is also an international lecturer on marketing, public relations and advertising at conferences and seminars.

ALSO IN THIS SERIES

Contents

Introduction

The cost of media is continually rising. Competitive activity in every market sector intensifies by the day. Both these factors make it ever tougher to ensure your message cuts effectively through the noise to reach your target customer. Paradoxically, as product differences continue to narrow and more companies fight for your customers' money, communication – meaningful, effective communication – plays an increasingly important role in business success.

Indeed, in many categories, there are only two real points of differentiation between competing brands: speed of response and power of communication – and that applies in both consumer and business markets. Genuine product superiority is relatively rare. The nature of modern business has driven weak products and brands out of the market; those that are left are, almost invariably, worthy competitors.

Even where a real difference exists, it is likely to be short term: your opponents will soon launch their own variant of your innovation.

An analysis of successful companies and brands shows a number of factors in common. Other books have covered many of them, from the search for excellence, through the drive for zero defects, to 'fifth generation' management and employee empowerment. Yet one key aspect is rarely written about in depth: every one of those successful businesses adopts an integrated approach to communication.

Consider BMW, Compaq, Coca Cola, Nikon, Tango, Sony, Sainsbury or Orange. These span markets from fast moving consumer goods (fmcg), through durables to business products. They cover extremes in terms of the value and the usage life of the purchase. But they are very similar in their commitment to consistency in their communication. As a result, they have clear and easily identifiable positionings and brand personalities. We know what we'll get from these brands – beyond the tangible product or service. The brand has built a relationship with its market. That relationship makes it harder for competitors to dislodge the brand and to create preference for their own products.

THE BENEFITS OF INTEGRATION

There are two main benefits of adopting such an integrated approach. The first is perhaps best illustrated by analogy.

We all have acquaintances whom we meet only occasionally. Imagine meeting one of your own social circle, let's say three times over the space of a few weeks. The first time you see them, they're wearing business clothes and discussing items of shared interest. The second, they're dressed as a Rastafarian and speaking in a Caribbean accent. The third, they've become a New Age traveller and are eulogising the benefits of living outside conventional society.

What opinion would you form of them? All three persona are perfectly common these days. If you saw such individuals in the street, you probably wouldn't find any of them particularly remarkable. But such inconsistency in a single individual would be disturbing, to say the least.

Our target customers meet our brands relatively infrequently (unless we're among those privileged few with huge communication budgets). If the brand is 'dressed' differently or speaks in a new accent every time the customer meets them, they too will be disturbed by the meeting. They'll be left with no clear view of what the company, brand and product means to them. Unless that's the result we seek, it cannot be good for business.

Communication which has a clear knowledge of what it aims to convey, and does so consistently over time, avoids that danger and allows us to build the kind of relationships which win customers and keep them. However, mere consistency is not enough. Consistent invisibility is of no great benefit! We do need to be distinctive and to maximise the number of contacts we have with our target if we are to be truly successful.

The second benefit relates to money. Consistent communication actually costs significantly less than ever-changing campaigns. At a practical level, we can often generate a single set of material – such as photographs – which then has multiple applications. That's a straight cost saving in production. The more important financial benefit however, lies in how much further we can make our budget stretch. Consistent communication creates a build-up effect. It's rather like any form of learning: regular reinforcement of a consistent message creates long-lasting knowledge. This makes it easier to maintain the brand message, and at lower cost.

The use of a combination of marketing communication techniques gives more opportunity to increase the number of times we 'meet' our customer. The build-up effect of delivering the same message through several media or techniques adds to the efficiency of our transmission. So, although it can be difficult to measure the effect precisely, we get more value from our investment.

WHO IS RESPONSIBLE?

Quite simply: *you* are. The protection of a brand and the integration of its communication should be the single most important function of any communication specialist; it is the most valuable task you can perform for your company.

In reality, brand protection is frequently left to the advertising agency. Marketers tend to change jobs fairly frequently and every new incumbent has to learn what the brand is and what the characteristics are which make it of value to its market. Agencies are better geared to capturing and verbalising this information. They will often hold a brand 'bible' which defines such elements of the brand.

This information should reside within the company itself.

External agencies are less than perfect at driving integration. A company using more than one agency – for example an advertising and a PR agency – will often experience tension between the two as they fight for share of available budget. This is not to suggest that these agencies do not believe the advice they are offering but is merely a reflection of human nature: their staff want to develop their own businesses and cannot be completely objective about such issues.

The proverbial 'buck' stops with the head of communication within the client company. True integration cannot and should not be delegated.

ABOUT THIS BOOK

I have set out to argue the case for integrated communication, whether for a company as a whole or for a specific brand. The book looks at what integrated communication is and how to go about developing the approach for your own products and services. It is not a scientific manual; there are no absolutely right answers because our understanding of how communication works is less than perfect – despite extensive research on the subject.

However, I am certain that an integrated approach will out-score a fragmented approach every time and deliver more effective and profitable communication.

The lessons are ones which should be known and understood by anyone who controls communication, whether in selling to businesses or domestic consumers, whether selling products or services, whether in large or small businesses.

1

What does Integrated Communication Mean?

We can claim that our communications are fully integrated when we have identified a single, core message which leads to one great creative idea which is implemented across everything we do. We maintain integrated communication over time when developments of our campaigns can be seen to be true to the positioning and personality of the brand.

Thus, for example, the Avis car rental company's 'We try harder' campaign ran for several years and a review of its elements over that time show a clear and deliberately controlled consistency of approach, tone of voice and message. The result was a clear position-ing in the minds of its target business audience: because we're only number two worldwide, we make an extra effort to win and keep your business.

In the consumer market, Levi jeans have carved a place in the minds of most of us. Their communication, spanning TV and cinema commercials, newspaper and magazine advertising, in-store promo-tion and many other techniques always delivers the same core message. That communication is instantly identifiable wherever we see or hear it. And that's a key measure of successful integration.

The purpose of any marketing communication is to deliver a clearly defined message to an identified target audience in an effect-ive manner. To do that for any company or brand, it is important to understand the hierarchy of communication, as shown in Figure 1.1.

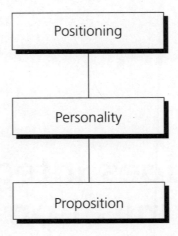

Figure 1.1 *A communication hierarchy*

Definitions of these stages abound. In simple terms, the positioning is *what* we want people to feel, the personality is *how* we want them to feel about the brand, and the proposition is how we believe we can bring about the other two. We'll return to this in Chapter 2. In integrating any campaign, these are our anchors; everything we do, every campaign we run, every message we send must be referred back to this chart. If we are confident it fits the descriptions we have established for each of these stages, then it passes the first test.

At this point we have integration at the intellectual level. Now we must check the proposed transmission (in whichever forms we intend to use) to ensure it looks and feels like the brand. These more physical elements represent the second test.

Both tests must be applied to each aspect of a campaign. In a smaller company, the temptation is to rely on our own judgement in running these checks. This is false economy. The only people capable of saying whether a proposed activity is true to the nature of the brand is the prospective customer. Even a relatively small amount invested in research to ask the market can pay significant dividends – and prevent our own subjectivity from leading us off course.

AMBUSH THE CUSTOMER!

There are times when each of us actively seeks advertising or promotional messages from suppliers: the man who wants to buy a second-hand car will avidly scour the smallest of advertisements in publications like *Auto Trader* or *Exchange & Mart*. However, most of the time we are not in the market for a given product The communication challenge is therefore to keep our brand at the forefront of the prospective customer's mind, and associated with appropriate images, so that we have an advantageous start at the time he or she does become an active buyer.

This is no small task when we bear in mind the sheer amount of commercial communication to which we are exposed. Research has claimed that each of us sees or hears as many as 1500 advertising messages each day. In preparing to write this book, I noted carefully those which I experienced over the course of a few days. Figure 1.2 shows the average daily exposure.

Posters	68
Radio commercials	26
Newspaper ads	35
Magazine ads	28
TV commercials	32
TOTAL	189

Figure 1.2 *Author's average daily advertising exposure*

In compiling this total, I ignored point-of-sale messages (and I work in central London!), editorial mentions of companies or brands, sponsorships messages, direct mail pieces and classified and recruitment advertising. Even without the rest of these attacks on my senses, I am being faced with almost 70,000 advertising messages each year. If I'm in your target market, how do you cut through that noise and make *your* message the one that sticks?

Naturally, there's no single, simple answer. The solution lies in a message reflecting a brand which offers a real benefit, delivered through a powerful creative idea, in a consistent manner – and often enough to make me remember it.

Few budgets can stand frequent enough transmission through advertising exclusively in order to have a major presence among those other 70,000 messages. Yet some brands seem to be omnipresent despite the restrictions of a viable budget. They achieve this by understanding how their market consumes media, then using the communications mix in a balanced package to deliver a concerted campaign. They will use one technique to lead the campaign, then 'ambush' the customer by using a whole range of other activities to increase the number of times we meet the brand (see Figure 1.3). And they'll deliver a single consistent message throughout these activities.

In other words, they adopt an integrated approach across all aspects of their communication and so achieve greater penetration for their message and a more efficient build-up of impact and retention.

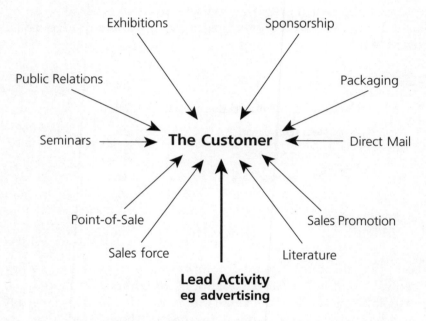

Figure 1.3 *Ambushing the customer*

CONSISTENCY ACROSS AUDIENCES – AND PRODUCTS

A campaign rarely needs to convince only one audience. Even in fast moving consumer goods, we need to persuade the trade to stock the product before we have a chance of success. In the case of a corporate campaign, we may find, in extreme cases, that we have to address many audiences ranging from staff and unions, through local authorities and the local community, to a multi-layered distribution network – and, of course, our target buyers.

Even in this extreme case, integration is possible. Indeed, its benefits are more significant when we tackle such a complex task. The positioning holds everything together. To use a hypothetical example: a chemicals company may define a positioning based around being the most innovative company in its sector. Its brand personality is dynamic and creative. Irrespective of the specific audience being addressed, every message it delivers must be couched in terms which reinforce that innovation.

For example, to a trade union, we might find phraseology such as 'Investment in a production line for our revolutionary new product means that . . .'; to the local community, 'thanks to a new technological breakthrough, we have reduced the environmental impact of our operation . . .' and so on. The specific message to be conveyed may concern restructuring, or new staff, or an investment programme, but each is delivered in a form which constantly reinforces the innovative nature of the company.

This applies equally across a range of products or services which may be elements of the brand or may be sub-brands in their own right. In our chemical company example, the particular benefits offered by a given product must be explained as arising from the innovative effort of the business. In the consumer durable market, Sony represents a good example of this type of integration working effectively. Their position is as an innovative company, delivering reliable products. The Trinitron sub-brand, applied to the tube technology in their TVs, benefits from the overall positioning, and it in turn supports that positioning.

Sony also demonstrates another useful spin-off from such a consistent positioning: the strength of its brand has allowed it to make mistakes without destroying its market position in the process.

Professional broadcasters will remember an unreliable professional video tape. Consumers will remember Betamax, the video system which ultimately failed to take the market. Yet we still trust the brand to deliver.

Such strength is not arrived at by accident. It is the direct result of a deliberate and considered approach to nurturing the brand, a process which demands an integrated strategy.

CONSISTENCY OVER TIME

Building a powerful brand cannot be done in five minutes. Consistency must be maintained over a long period before the brand becomes 'etched into' the minds of the target market. How long that takes is likely to be determined by the available budget. As we have seen on some of the privatisation launches in recent years, it is possible to intrude on the collective brain relatively quickly – as we might have 'told Sid' during the British Gas share launch. But that level of penetration of a large part of the UK population costs several million pounds over a short period. Many of us now face global audiences in our businesses. That gives some idea of the scale of the challenge we face – and further reinforces the need to make every penny deliver a result.

There are many classic examples of advertising campaigns (usually the most visible element of communication) which have really stuck to the task: PG Tips, Holsten Pils, Compaq Computers, Orange to name but a few.

Notice, too, that integrated communication does not mean boring or unchanging communication. In the case of each of those mentioned, we have seen numerous specific campaigns over the years, all of which have displayed high standards of creativity. Each stands out as memorable in its particular market sector. Each has shown variety in how the message was delivered. Yet all have remained true to the core positioning and personality of the brand – only the campaign proposition has changed over time.

It is worth noting that there are apparent exceptions to the rule. Lucozade is a case in point. The brand was always something you took along for a sick relative, or gave an ailing child. It was associated with youth and illness. However, today Lucozade is right up to date, a brand for the nineties.

This is certainly a fundamental – and successful – shift in both positioning and personality. But it, too, is a fine example of integrated communication. The brand owner realised a new marketing strategy was needed to prevent the death of the brand. Research helped define a new positioning relevant to modern consumers, as a health drink. From then on, everything about the brand, or associated with it, was designed to deliver the new positioning. From the packaging design to the advertising, each element was developed to build a new place in the market for what had become almost a commercial liability.

IS INTEGRATION ALWAYS NECESSARY?

The short answer is yes and no! The guideline is simple: if we are discussing a single brand, then everything associated with that brand must be fully integrated in support of the brand's positioning and personality. Therefore the basis of the decision must be a clear identification of our brands.

In consumer marketing, this is generally fairly easy. In the automotive market for example, we see single brands such as BMW, where individual models are numbered for identification and Ford, where each model is a sub-brand in its own right. Both promote individual models but the communication tasks are slightly different in that all BMW models must conform rigidly to the brand personality whereas the Ford products can have more of an individual personality – although conforming to the core characteristics of the umbrella brand of the parent. Similarly, in the soft drinks market, Schweppes' products are subsidiary to the main brand while Britvic is virtually invisible in its Tango brand. Such consumer marketers have sophisticated branding policies which are usually very well established.

The position is a bit more complex in business-to-business marketing. Here, the company is often the brand – specific product brands being the exception rather than the rule. However, in looking at such 'corporate' brands, the level of integration necessary will vary with the extent of the corporation's activities.

The key lies in looking from the market's viewpoint. Where there is a consistency of audience, integration is essential. Figure 1.4 shows the example of a corporation made up of parent and several subsidiary companies. The circles represent the businesses' total audiences.

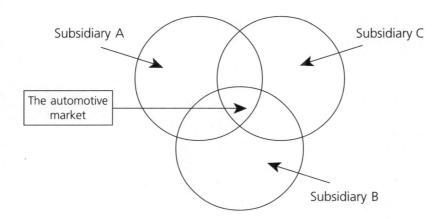

Figure 1.4 *Overlap in target audiences among sister companies*

All of the companies sell into the automotive market – although each has a number of other markets in addition. If the automotive market is important to the business as a whole, one would conclude that such a coincidence of audience dictates that communication should be integrated throughout the corporation. By contrast, in a diversified conglomerate where the subsidiary companies are each addressing different markets, the only common audiences are at corporate level: shareholders, analysts and so on. Arguably, there are few major benefits to be had from integration in such a case and each subsidiary could reasonably be treated as a brand in its own right.

2

Planning for Integration

Any effective communication is the outcome of structured thinking combined with insight into the needs, aspirations and attitudes of the target customer. If we don't have these, integration is academic since our communication is more than likely to be off-target in any event.

The start and end points of our thinking must be the customer. As Figure 2.1 shows, the process starts with our understanding of the market's wants and needs. This knowledge allows us to define a meaningful positioning. A segmentation of our total audience enables us to identify which messages must be communicated to each, which gives us a planning matrix. Now that we have defined precisely the task facing us, we can develop a strategy to deliver the messages effectively. From the strategy we can define and execute the individual tactical activities. Finally, the process ends with an evaluation of how well our communication has worked in the customers' eyes. We feed back what we have learned in a constant cycle of review and refinement which helps us increase the effectiveness of our communication over time.

TOWARDS A POSITIONING

Whether we like it or not, our products, services, brands and indeed our company will, through our activities and corporate behaviour, generate an image in the minds of our customers and prospects.

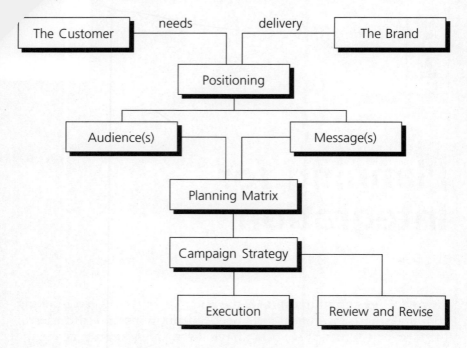

Figure 2.1 *Planning for integration*

The only option we have is whether or not to manage the development or alteration of that image. If we choose not to do so, at best we fail to exploit our potential. In the worst case, we leave ourselves highly vulnerable to sharper competitors who are more in tune with the market.

A positioning can be described as a definition of the core characteristic of the brand which we believe will differentiate it in its market and which will motivate people to select it in preference to competing brands. It is an encapsulation of what we want our audience to think, feel and believe about the brand. It is an essential prerequisite to integrated communication since it provides the single focus around which every aspect of our communication will be constructed. Without a clear positioning, there can be no true integration.

As we see in Figure 2.1, an effective positioning stems from two elements: the needs of our market, and what our brand delivers. If we cannot find a match between these two, we have no real positioning.

The needs of our market

The basis for everything is an understanding of the n
does the customer seek from our particular category?
powder market, for example, the key motivators may li
two areas:

1. a rational belief that the powder washes whiter; and
2. an emotional need to feel that using the product makes us a better
   parent or more caring partner.

In the business computer market, our rational demand may be
higher data handling capacity or improved personal productivity.
Our emotional need could be to be seen as modern, or as being senior
in the organisation ('I'm the one with the multi-media laptop.').

No market is made up of clones, therefore our understanding must
reach beyond simple generalisations into a knowledge of the key
segments within our market. And we'll need to be confident that
we're addressing a segment which is big enough to give us a fair
chance of meeting our business objectives. I think it was David
Bernstein who said, 'We know there's a gap in the market, but is
there a market in the gap?'

Finding out what our market is about is not easy. We are not
dealing simply with how our prospective customers voice their
conscious opinions on our product or market area; we need also
to reach into their collective psyche and identify the unspoken
emotions which lead to selection of a specific brand. We may get
some idea of these emotions through feedback if we have a
particularly good salesforce or distribution network, but even their
opinions will rarely go beyond the rational reasoning process.
(Indeed, in many cases the salesforce rarely meets an end consumer,
dealing only with the distribution network.)

To reach those subconscious aspirations and desires, there is no
substitute for properly conducted research, usually involving a mix
of personal and group interviews with members of the target
audience. This process can help us narrow our target market
definition and sharpen our marketing as a result. It is certainly of
major benefit in leading us towards the optimum positioning for
what we have to offer.

In researching the market we aim to build a picture of those key
segments and the main motivators in each. The result should be a
kind of 'league table' of needs and aspirations, as shown in Figure
2.2. Those needs and aspirations – the key motivators – are rated in

Target Segment	Key Motivator	Competitive Edge
1	1 2 3	1 2 3
2	1 2 3	1 2 3
3	1 2 3	1 2 3

Figure 2.2 *Identifying the positioning options*

a priority order for each segment we propose to address. There are few market sectors where there is only one motivator – one of the reasons why several major players can exist in a particular sector. However, the sort of in-depth understanding recommended here will identify a specific main motivator in each segment. In fact, using motivators as the basis for marketing segmentation can be highly effective in itself.

What our brand delivers

When we understand what the market is really 'buying', we can turn to what we have to offer. What are the main benefits which we can offer the market? If we have them, unique benefits go to the top of the list. After those, we should concentrate on areas where we have a competitive advantage, and list them in order of competitive power – perhaps by scoring them from 1 to 5 depending on how much better we are in that area than our main competitors.*

In an ideal scenario, the area where we have the best competitive position would match precisely the motivator at the top of our customer needs list. We would position our brand around that issue. If this is not the case, as in most instances, then we must look at our next strongest area, and so on, until we find a match.

---

* Note that, for the purpose of explaining these steps, I have assumed we are looking at an existing product.

This process is more difficult than it first appears. In many markets, the marketer is faced with promoting 'me too' products with little to distinguish them in any rational sense. And this is where our customer understanding is truly critical to our chances of success.

The history of the *Häagen Dazs* ice cream brand is particularly enlightening on this point. The opportunity was seen to launch a premium product made with 'real' ingredients to compete with the major, highly-processed ice creams which dominated the market. The original positioning was around better taste and an imaginative range of unusual flavours. Everything was developed to deliver the positioning, including the brand name. *Häagen Dazs* is a marketing invention, which gives a feeling of being vaguely foreign and exotic, and of being long established.

The brand was very successful. It established a strong adult following, unlike most ice creams which were perceived as being for children. Inevitably the brand spawned imitators which challenged its market share. The brand owner's response was to position the brand even more strongly towards its rather avant-garde adult market. Today, it has moved from being merely a premium ice cream to being sex in a tub. It is promoted as a highly sensual eating experience, illustrated by the 'beautiful people' featured in its advertising and other communications.

This case is significant. The brand was losing the logical, rational basis of its positioning to rising competition. It re-established its ascendancy through its understanding of the emotional elements of the purchase inherent in its key segments.

So, in preparing the type of analysis illustrated in Figure 2.2, we must take a holistic view of the brand and give appropriate weighting to what we can offer emotionally as well as rationally. If we become too focused on the physical characteristics of our offer, we are likely to miss some of the more important positioning options.

If one of our top three benefits coincides with one of our market's top three needs, our positioning is likely to be strong enough to let us capture a significant share of our particular target segment. If not, we should question whether we should be investing scarce communication funds in this particular brand. Perhaps the wiser investment would be in developing the brand to deliver something which the market really wants. (In the case where we propose to develop a new product to fulfil a perceived market gap, we would match our development abilities to the customer needs and then design a product or service which had the potential to take the high ground in one particular area of motivation.)

This type of analysis can apply to a product brand, a range brand or even a company brand. Current examples of successful positioning would include Tango, the orange drink with more of the 'zing' we demand of a sweet, aerated soft drink, Zanussi with its 'appliance of science' theme capitalising on a desire for labour-saving modern technology, and Volvo which appeals to a certain segment of the car market through its safety positioning.

It may even be possible, although it is relatively rare, to create a *new* motivator through technological advance. Radion, the washing powder, was formulated specifically to give a smell of freshness after the wash and was positioned as not only washing clothes but also killing any residual smells. With its Walkman, Sony went even further and created a new market – the motivators in such a case actually follow the launch of the first product in the new category.

Repositioning can also save failing brands, as in the case of Lucozade quoted in Chapter 1.

Where we are marketing a brand which covers a single product, we can progress directly to developing a campaign strategy from this point. Frequently, however, the brand covers a range of products or services, or is a corporate brand in which case the positioning must hold good for the company as a whole.

THE FEATURES OF A BROADER POSITIONING

The approach to identifying a positioning in such a case is basically the same as already described. However, instead of looking at a fairly narrow product category, we seek to find the motivators in a whole market sector – as the Swatch brand has done in watches – or even across a whole industry – for example, Hitachi in the electronic components market.

Here we demand even more of the positioning statement. The challenge now becomes that of finding a positioning which is broad enough to cover all of our offer but still sharp enough to give us a base for competitive advantage. Against such a broad requirement you are likely to be faced with a number of positioning options. Therefore we must examine what the attributes of a strong positioning are and assess each option against those attributes. Figure 2.3 gives a checklist of attributes which generally apply, against which to assess alternative positions.

If it is to help us establish competitive strength, a positioning must display a number of characteristics, discussed below.

	1	2	3	4	5
Strategic					
Single-minded					
Customer-led					
Deliverable					
Broad-shouldered					
High ground					
Distinctive					
Sustainable					
Motivating					
Catalytic					

Figure 2.3 *Comparing positioning options*
(Courtesy of Ogilvy & Mather)

Strategic

Positioning must be strategic in nature, not a short-term solution or simply a basis for advertising. We would never, for example, position a company as offering the fastest delivery in its market just because its competitors were suffering a short-term supply problem. (Although, at a tactical level, this might be a particular message we want to communicate – under the umbrella of the overall positioning.)

Single-minded

It is hard enough to transmit one clear positioning in any cost-effective manner against all of the competitive 'noise' which assaults our target market. To compound the problem by trying to establish a multi-aspect positioning is both expensive and dangerous. The expense is obvious; the danger lies in confusing the audience.

Customer-led

This point applies particularly in business markets and hi-tech products. Marketers are frequently fascinated by the technologies with which they work. Regrettably for them, the market rarely shares that same enthusiasm.

In the early days of personal computers, the market was made up of a relatively small number of what might be described as 'techno freaks'. They loved all of the technical data on the inner workings of the product. The hi-fi and professional camera markets displayed the same characteristics. However, as such products fell in price and disposable incomes rose, these markets changed – and so did the audiences. It would be risky today to position such products purely around technical features.

The common error in industrial markets is to position company brands entirely around the products, thus ignoring the real influence of emotional issues in business buying. The key is to ensure that the positioning is developed from a customer-led view.

Deliverable

We must be able to justify the product rationally, or near rationally before it will be acceptable to the market. Thus it must be born of our areas of strength. Audi's claim of 'Vorsprung durch Technik' would have no credibility if the cars were not seen to be a result of progress through technology; in other words, if they lacked the technical refinement of competitive models. The Avis claim of 'We try harder' falls down quickly unless customers actually experience a genuine drive for superior service. However, the reality is often not quite so clear-cut.

We don't consciously believe that all cowboys smoked Marlboro cigarettes for all those years. Yet the product attributes are such that we could *imagine* cowboys smoking them – and that unconscious willingness to accept the positioning is the key to its success. It's easy to see from such an example just how important the understanding of our consumer is.

Broad-shouldered

This is the point where a multi-product or a company brand differs significantly from that for a single product or service. Such an umbrella brand must, by definition, be capable of covering a wider range of activities. Although the analysis process doesn't change as a result, in many respects it becomes more difficult.

We now have to analyse customer needs on a broader basis. What is it that makes a loyal Ford or BMW driver, who will trade up from model to model throughout a lifetime? It may be more understandable – at least in terms of brand values – in the BMW case since their promotion is focused on the marque rather than the model. That doesn't explain, however, why a driver will move from a Fiesta to an Escort to a Mondeo. Nor, to betray my age, does it explain why many stayed with the Cortina through four very different models; indeed, through four entirely different cars.

It is essential, in searching for this umbrella positioning, to find the broad issues which are important to the market. In computing, it may be an overall ability to up-grade the products easily. Equally, as Toshiba could testify, it may be about carrying a laptop with a certain cachet.

This type of brand is very common in business marketing. But it's equally common in the High Street: every supermarket brand would qualify. What aspect of pricing, convenience or self-image leads to your choice of where to shop?

High ground

As with all of these points, this relates back to the hierarchy of motivators in the market. Any brand positioning needs to be capable of capturing the mind. It must therefore capture at least some area of the available 'high ground.'

The main motivator in the soap powder market may well be the ability to wash clothes clean. It is doubtful that a brand positioned merely as 'getting clothes clean' would make much of a dent in competitors' shares.

Distinctive

We seek a positioning that's different from our competitors'. There is little point in investing in building a 'me too' position in the market. If a competitor has done a good job, there's a real danger that we'd be spending money more to their benefit rather than our own. It's hard to imagine another lager being positioned as 'refreshing' with any real hope of dislodging Heineken from that slot. Or of another soft drink beating Coca-Cola as 'the real thing'.

As is evident from this and other points, a sound knowledge of competition is an essential ingredient in developing the positioning.

Sustainable

The positioning must not only be supportable today, it must be sustainable over time. 'Time' is not, however, an absolute commodity in marketing. We must relate our definition of it to the likely life of the brand. If we are in the market for the relative short term, then a year or two may be enough. However, brands of that nature are rare these days; it costs so much to build a powerful brand that we need it to have a long life if we are to recoup our investment with a profit.

So we need to ensure any positioning has the legs to run for several years. For example, if a paper mill chose to market its products under one 'umbrella' brand, it would be foolish to build the brand positioning around the use of the very latest technology. Mills are built to pay back over 20 years or more and updating is an infrequent and costly process. A mill built just a year or two later would probably use more sophisticated technology – invalidating the position of our imaginary brand almost overnight and necessitating investment in repositioning.

Similarly, positioning a brand around innovation just because the company has launched one revolutionary product is fraught with problems. Conversely, an organisation such as AT&T, with its Nobel Laboratories registering literally hundreds of patents every year, could substantiate an 'innovation' positioning and maintain it over time.

We must be sure, when we choose an area of competitive edge as a basis for brand building, that it has long-term validity.

Motivating

Perhaps the single most important aspect of any positioning is that it must motivate our potential customers to prefer our brand over that of our competitors. Any positioning must therefore be clearly based on the audience motivations we have unearthed in research; it should, ideally, capture both the emotional and rational aspects of selection.

This point is closely allied with the need to be customer-led. A modern 'point and click' camera with auto everything built in certainly uses technology every bit as sophisticated as a professional

Hasselblad camera – but could never be directly positioned on the basis of that technology since it is not what the 'point and click' market cares about. The technology story may well be a powerful substantiation of the positioning but it is not the lead element.

Catalytic

Since this is a book on communication, we must not miss one last and important qualifier: does the proposed positioning look as if it could spark some top-notch creative solutions?

If a positioning does not act as a catalyst to powerful, intrusive campaigns then it is in danger of remaining a closely guarded secret!

Using Figure 2.3 as a checklist allows us to eliminate the obvious failures and to narrow our focus down to one or two strong candidates. If the issue is not resolved at this point, it may be necessary to develop several written statements summarising variants of each option, then take these back to the market.

Even if a clear winner has emerged from the process this latter stage is a good insurance policy prior to committing funds to campaign development. Experienced qualitative researchers can test the positioning statements and give a good indication as to which are likely to be most effective in the marketplace.

BE AWARE OF BRAND PERSONALITY

Personality is a difficult subject to put down on paper, yet it is easy to illustrate by example. Let me list several brands and allow you to examine your own reaction to those you know:

▪ Virgin
▪ Arthur Andersen
▪ Amstrad
▪ Flora
▪ Kwiksave
▪ Bang & Olufsen
▪ British Airways
▪ Sainsbury
▪ JVC

I have deliberately chosen a range from business through consumer durable, to fmcg brands. The list includes manufacturers and distributors. And you will, no doubt, have noticed one or two competing brands. How would you describe each?

You may share some of my own views. I see Virgin as younger and livelier than British Airways, but a bit brash. Flora is older and a bit staid. B&O is for older, richer and more style-driven consumers than is JVC. Kwiksave is for those who can't afford the more exotic choice offered at Sainsbury. Amstrad is pushy, cheap and downmarket. Arthur Andersen is intellectual, thorough and very upmarket as a business brand.

These are of course value judgements made from my own personal perspective, and I intend no criticism in making them. Indeed, if I am not in the target market, or among those whose opinions can influence that market, then my views are totally irrelevant.

What my reactions and your own illustrate yet again is that each brand has more than just a rational basis for the image we form. It has a personality which is uniquely its own, a personality which goes beyond many positioning statements. When we research market motivations, competitor research should identify the personalities of other brands in our sector. We need to define our target personality as the last stage in pinning down our positioning.

As I write, I am in the middle of a positioning exercise for a product related to home security. Its rational positioning is clear: it makes domestic houses more secure than any current or envisaged product in its particular sector. It is valid, sustainable at least for the foreseeable future and meets most of the other criteria examined earlier. But the phrasing is cold; it lacks emotional appeal – and personality.

Emotionally, what the brand can offer is that intangible feeling of reduced threat to home and family. However, that is itself a somewhat negative expression of the emotion. Our team took one step further in seeking to breathe a warm, friendly personality into the brand. The outcome was the proposition briefed to the creative team, summed up simply as 'Happy Castles'.

This very brief statement captures the rational reason to buy but also adds the emotional warmth which understands what people want from such products. It is very different from the 'macho' personality normally associated with security products. It is a good example of how the insight to be gained from research leads to an effective positioning which clearly differentiates the brand from its competitors. And which in turn leads to a proposition that will act as a catalyst for an imaginative creative solution.

It is perhaps easier to understand this aspect of positioning in the context of a consumer product, but it also applies, for example, to services sold to businesses.

The following is a hypothetical example of developing a personality for a communications company brand offering some form of managed service such as the integration of several technologies into one network.

Rational attributes:
- Established and financially sound
- Known in this market, good reputation
- Relevant skills and people
- Good references across a range of blue-chip clients.

Emotional attributes:
- Friendly
- Easy to deal with
- Bright, challenging
- Pushes the boundaries.

Such information could have been gathered or confirmed by research among existing customers. They can help us establish the facts of our 'reality' and thus a sound basis for positioning the company. The picture they give is of a company which is innovative and challenging rather than a 'safe' choice. For that reason they will never be everyone's ideal business partner. The segment they are likely to have most success with consists of decision makers who are prepared to take a calculated risk by using the latest technological solutions, rather than the more conservative types who will wait until the solution is proven elsewhere.

A match between aspirations in the market and what the company delivers might lead to a positioning statement along the lines of: 'Integrated solutions for those who create the future.' Their target segment probably see themselves as mould-breakers and such a statement would trigger empathy with that self-image but, at the same time, prospects would rationalise the appeal by quoting the 'integrated solutions' element.

Such a statement in a business market also captures the personality of the brand. It is innovative in delivering its solutions. It breaks the rules to find new ways of doing things. It paints a picture of 'creative rebels' in a positive way.

If our brand covers what is in effect a single product, we could go directly from this stage to constructing a communication strategy since the positioning and personality add up to the proposition for the campaign. If, however, it is a positioning which must cover a range of products or services, or even a whole company, we need to turn the positioning into a series of related product or service propositions, tailored to specific parts of our total audience. This aspect is covered in more depth in Chapter 4.

3

The Planning Matrix

In this chapter the most complex of scenarios is used to illustrate the development of a planning matrix. The example is that of preparing a plan for a major multinational with numerous products and geographic units. The approach is equally valid, and much easier to implement, in a smaller company.

The key is to do as any good communication plan must do, which is to mirror the structure of the company, and the business and marketing objectives at each level. The example used is that of a real company but for reasons of confidentiality its identity is not given. It is an industrial company operating across the globe. Its many products are sold into many industries.

In Figure 3.1 we see the main planning levels within the organisation. The company is structured around business units, one for each strategically important area of its business. In parallel it has a number of functional divisions such as manufacturing and personnel. The business unit structure is customer-led, selling to two broad categories: applications of its products and services which run across a number of industries, and 'vertically' with a range of appropriate products into specific industries. It also operates a regional sales structure with particular geographic responsibilities. This structure is now relatively common in the more customer-led companies.

Our first aim is to understand the business and marketing objectives at each level. That understanding is then used to identify which audiences are important to achieving the objectives at each level. Finally, key messages are defined for each relevant audience.

The end result is a matrix, or perhaps several matrices, which match audiences and messages in a way which helps identify campaign structure.

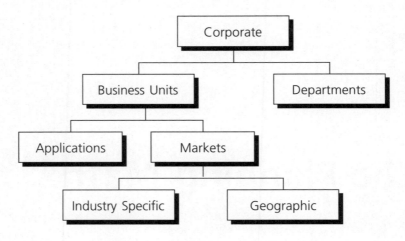

Figure 3.1 *The various planning levels*

CORPORATE AUDIENCES

The mission statement, long-term plan and annual budget contain the objectives for the corporation as a whole. We need to look closely at each key objective and apply the question 'who can help or hinder us in getting there?'

The answer is likely to comprise numerous audiences, from staff, through suppliers, regulatory authorities, local and national government and trade unions, to stock market analysts and shareholders. Depending on the objectives we may also need to reach, for example, acquisition targets or potential purchasers of businesses we wish to sell. At this point these audiences should be listed in priority order based on their ability to affect the achievement of the plan. This will help to construct a viable budget at a later stage as we are rarely able to afford to do everything we would wish.

It is now possible to use a similar process to that used to identify the brand positioning. In this case, we seek to match the major issues in the minds of each audience with what we can deliver against those issues. If, for example, regulators are currently deeply concerned about environmental performance, we need to communicate the positive aspects of our performance in that area. Again, it is useful to pose a question against each key audience: 'what must they feel or believe if we are to succeed?'

In Figure 3.2 we see a notional matrix based on the corporate analysis. As we enter the crosses to identify which messages go to which audiences, a pattern starts to emerge. By the time we have finished this whole exercise, the various patterns will point us towards the campaigns we should be producing.

BUSINESS AUDIENCES

At the next level down, we repeat the process asking the same questions of ourselves. For the business units we will need to define audiences from more than one perspective. We need to identify which applications areas (machine tools for turning work, for example) we will attack as part of the plan. This might lead us to a broad 'horizontal' audience of machine tool specifiers – irrespective of which industry they are in. However, it might be that the auto-motive industry is of particular importance if we are to reach our objectives, in which case this needs to be specified and the key decision makers in that industry identified as targets. Finally, particular countries or regions could be crucial to the future and these, too, should be dealt with.

In a large, multi-product business unit, it may be necessary to subdivide the analysis into several matrices to avoid the process becoming too cumbersome.

At an early stage, the priority market, application and product areas should be identified – indeed, they should have been in the business or marketing plan – and since they are the keys to the plan, analysis should be restricted to these. Again, this keeps the process to a manageable level.

DEPARTMENTAL AUDIENCES

Exactly the same approach is applied to the specialist functions. In a fast-growing company, recruitment of quality staff might be a critical factor: potential candidates become a prime audience for the personnel or human resources department. An efficient computer network could be important, so the information technologists might have their own target audiences.

As before, each of the business and functional audiences must be considered and appropriate messages identified.

Message \ Audience	A	B	C	D	E	F
Good employers	X		X	X		X
Good neighbours		X	X			
Well managed		X				X
Honest and open	X	X	X		X	

Figure 3.2 *A corporate audience/message matrix*

ASSEMBLING THE PLAN

Now the real task of integrating our communication can begin.

Examine each of the matrices, looking for repetition of audiences. There will almost certainly be several mentions of employees. This is a sadly neglected audience in many companies, yet staff are fundamental to everything a company does. Keeping them informed and motivated, and ensuring they feel they have a personal part to play in achieving the objectives should be a significant task in any communications plan. In a company run through a series of business units, there are also likely to be cases of more than one unit addressing a specific industry. Certainly where a geographic region is important, a number of units will identify that region as a focus for activity.

The matrices can therefore be reassembled from the point of view of the receivers of our communication. Identify key audiences and prepare a matrix along the lines of Figure 3.3 for each.

The revised perspective really highlights the need for integration in communication. A number of important audiences will be reached by messages from several sources within the company. If there is no consistency in those messages, there is little chance of transmitting a picture of the organisation which makes sense to that particular audience. As we will see later, in Chapter 5, the position becomes worse when we begin to select media. With few exceptions, the media which we have available to transmit our communication are not so selective as our own targeting. Thus when targeting one segment of our audience we will almost certainly reach others. Integration of the content of this communication is essential to avoid confusion.

Audience: ....

Message ╲ Source	A	B	C	D

Figure 3.3 *A plan matrix from the receiver's view*

IDENTIFYING THE CAMPAIGN STRUCTURE

Combining the two sets of information ┤ the company perspective and the audience perspective – allows us to identify the campaigns we need to execute to meet the objectives.

It should be evident from the information that there must be, for example, an employee campaign, an automotive industry campaign and a major campaign in the Asia Pacific region. We also know which messages each campaign must deliver in order to do the job. The list of campaigns may still be overwhelming. Take the red pen and question yet again whether each is genuinely necessary and strike out those which cannot be clearly shown to be so.

In a large organisation, the campaigns can now be structured to reflect the shape of the business and a one-page summary made of the total task. Figure 3.4 shows an example. This may need to be supported with a second sheet giving outline information on required, shorter term tactical campaigns. In a smaller business the same format can be used with the content tailored appropriately.

We have now defined the tasks which communication must fulfil. This is no small achievement; the process produces a meaningful strategy with the optimum chance of making a real contribution to achieving the corporate and business unit objectives.

Core Campaigns		Key Audiences	Geography		
			USA	Europe	Asia
Corporate	1				
	2				
Functional	1				
	2				
	3				
Business Unit	1				
	2				
	3				
Product	1				
	2				
	3				

Figure 3.4 *Summary campaign structure for a large company*

MANAGING THE PROCESS

In a small or a highly centralised company, process management is relatively easy. In a larger business, or more especially in one with decentralised decision making, it is much more difficult. However, in either case it is not a one-person job.

Communication is essential to develop a meaningful communication plan. Extensive discussion is needed at each level and at each stage. The corporate elements must be agreed at senior level so the communication department has a real understanding of the broad company objectives, and so the board has confidence in the final proposal; if they are committed, they will help make it happen (and be somewhat slower to cut the budget half-way through). Business unit marketing staff and functional management must be heavily involved in their respective parts – in a devolved organisation, they will be responsible for the ultimate execution and must understand and commit to integration if they are to have any chance of bringing it to fruition.

Such a shared process has immense benefit when final decisions are made to proceed; some parts of the programme will, almost inevitably, be cut in order to work within a viable budget. If everyone of consequence understands the process and its purpose, the communications manager will suffer much less from in-fighting when those cuts become necessary. When the need for full integration is understood and accepted, there is a lower incidence of the 'not invented here' syndrome which is frequently seen, for example, in local units finding a dozen good reasons not to run centrally developed campaigns 'because they just won't work in our market'.

The ideal circumstance occurs when the communication plan is developed as a central element in the business planning process rather than as an adjunct to it, and when we carry our colleagues with us each step of the way.

In practical terms, we must recognise that not all of those colleagues are communication experts and that frequently they will not fully understand what we are trying to achieve through the planning process. It is the communication department's job to give them a clear understanding by explaining the need and the process being followed. But we can go further by preparing simple tools to help them give us the information we need in a form which makes it easy for us to work with.

STRATEGY SUMMARY **BUSINESS UNIT:** ....

Completed by: .... **PLAN PERIOD:** ....
Date: ....

Key business objectives	Main strategy	Key audiences	Geographic/timing limitations
Any specific communication activities required:			

Figure 3.5 *Form used to simplify planning issues*

One major problem is taking a long and involved corporate long-term plan and distilling out its essence so we can identify the communication need. Figure 3.5 shows a simple form used in a global company with a number of separate business units. It helps the business manager focus clearly on the priorities in a way which helps the communication specialist. It also recognises that he or she has valuable input to make, in that it provides space for the identification of exhibitions, literature requirements and so on, which the manager feels are important in the specific market. The use of such simple forms can make the whole process smoother and less onerous for all concerned.

4

Shaping Individual Campaigns

Having prepared the overall structure, we can begin to progress each individual campaign. Figure 4.1 shows the approach to be adopted. We begin with the marketing or business objective and the audience which must be addressed. The parameters of the campaign are specified – which priority industries, which countries and so on. We examine the current situation then define appropriate communication objectives. Finally, we decide on a strategy and a tactical plan to achieve them.

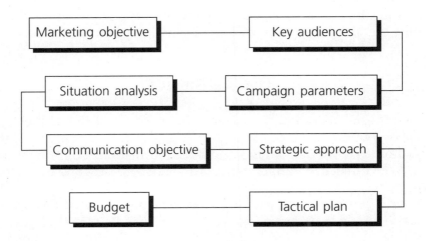

Figure 4.1 *Developing individual campaigns*

BUSINESS AND MARKETING OBJECTIVES

Business objectives are normally stated in purely financial terms, for example:

■ to achieve a return on capital employed of X per cent;
■ to increase turnover to £X and profit to £Y during the plan period;
■ to limit employee costs to X per cent of turnover.

They are usually derived using the key ratios which the company uses to run its business and measure its performance. Marketing objectives should address themselves more to *how* these figures are to be achieved, for example:

■ to increase sales of brand X by Y per cent in a specified market;
■ to establish an alternative distribution channel, delivering Y per cent of sales by the end of the plan period;
■ to increase market share of brand Y by X per cent in the period.

By their very nature, business and marketing objectives are tightly specified, measurable and limited by time – the characteristics of a real objective rather than simply a vague aim.

If we do not understand these objectives and the rationale behind them, it is almost impossible to produce an effective communication effort to support them. This appears to be a statement of the obvious yet, tragically, all too many marketing services departments are kept at arm's length from the central planning process and end up with only the flimsiest notion of what the company is trying to do.

KEY AUDIENCES

Once again, we fall back on our understanding of the market as a major foundation stone of our thinking. The earlier elements of the planning process should have put this information at our fingertips.

'Who can help or hinder us in reaching the business and marketing objectives?'

At campaign level, we need detailed knowledge of the people involved, their attitudes and aspirations and the part they play in the decision making for the product, service or brand. The following is the audience description for a new advertising medium launched in the mid-Nineties.

Our audience falls into two parts, agency media planners and senior marketing services personnel within client companies.

The media planners to be addressed are those in the top 100 agencies, who represent the vast majority of potential media purchases. They are relatively creative by instinct but were at the time all too aware of the significant reduction in their numbers caused by the recession. As a result, they were feeling conservative and reluctant to risk – as they saw it – spending already reduced client budgets outside proven mainstream media.

Client personnel had taken at least as much of a battering and were likely to be feeling equally conservative.

However, both audiences were frustrated by the limitations necessarily imposed to combat recession and were susceptible to something interesting and new which might brighten the dullness.

The key focus was media planners since one 'conversion' would reach a number of clients and they are key influencers of client decisions. However, we needed to predispose client personnel to being open to a proposal to test this new medium. They would be the ultimate decision makers.

The above is a synopsis of a much longer description but it contains the main elements. It gives us a feel for the task and market conditions. It tells us what attitudes the audience currently holds. And it identifies the role which each part of the audience plays in the decision.

The size of the decision making unit will vary enormously depending on the type of product or service involved. The number of people making up the decision making unit will, in general, increase as the value of the purchase under consideration increases. Thus a child's decision on which chocolate bar to buy with its pocket money will involve only the child. Buying a family car, however, will probably involve the whole family. At the other end of the scale, awarding a contract for the construction of a bridge or a power station could involve literally dozens of people, all of whom can influence a potential supplier's chances of success.

There are of course exceptions: the purchase of a 'singles' holiday is, almost by definition, a one-person decision in spite of the relatively large amount of money involved.

We must understand the dynamics involved in the decision. Even in the case of a family purchase there is not a standard pattern. Take two typical examples: a hi-fi system and a freezer. In both, the decision is likely to be taken jointly by the partners. However, they will play different roles in each case.

For the hi-fi system, both will be concerned about sound quality, the female partner will probably be more interested than the male in the aesthetics of the unit and how it will fit visually into the family home. The male will tend to be more concerned about the technical features on offer. That technical interest will also be seen in the purchase of a freezer. However, it will usually be the female partner who is really concerned about the practicality of the product – whether it suits her shopping or cooking patterns, how accessible food is once stored. But in these and many other categories of product, the blurring of gender is changing these somewhat stereo-typical roles.

These changes in the consumer market, and the complexity of the decision process in businesses make it essential that we really understand how the market buys – irrespective of which field of marketing we are involved in. Without such insight we cannot, with any confidence, define the messages which we must send.

CAMPAIGN PARAMETERS

We must understand clearly the limitations we are imposing on the extent of the particular campaign.

The audience definition will already give us some direction. It must identify the category or categories of consumer which we wish to reach; it must identify – in a business-to-business campaign – which industries and individuals we want to influence.

However, there may be further restrictions. What is the geography of the campaign? Are we addressing a local region, the whole country, a block of countries – such as ASEAN or the European Union – or are we faced with a truly global market? Within this geography we need to know if there is an order of priority, if partic-ular parts of our audience are critical to success. This will become important when we start to refine our activities to a viable level of budget.

Are there proven seasonal trends within the market in any or all of these areas? We must be familiar with sales variance during the year or planning period, and of the degree of fluctuation in those variances. Then we will know whether we have discrete periods of activity or merely periods when we can afford a lower level of activity than at others. The point is easily illustrated by comparing, for example, the market for New Year's greetings cards with that for 'Welcome to your new home' cards. The former has a very definitive, short selling season. Promotional activity at the wrong time would be virtually worthless. The latter cards are subject to seasonal variations in house moving – but there is always some activity in the market at any time of year and so a low level of promotional activity may well be highly appropriate.

In any company there will also be what we can regard as 'fixed' events which must be factored into our planning. Where stock market analysts are an identified audience, the Annual General Meeting of shareholders becomes such a fixed event. In a recruitment campaign, the end of the school or university year may be key. In almost every company there will be activities such as new product launches, factory or store openings, annual sales conferences, major industry exhibitions and so on, all of which must be taken into account. These, too, may be regarded as parameters for the campaign as well, of course, as elements of it.

All of this information helps narrow our focus further, thus ensuring that our – inevitably limited – communication budget is targeted at those market segments which offer the greatest potential in reaching our marketing and business objectives. It gives us the scope of our audience and, using data available from in-company and published sources (such as trade association and governmental statistics), allows us to define the size and location of that audience. When we add our knowledge of seasonal buying patterns and of our channels of distribution, we can develop a timing plan for when our activity needs to be at its highest for optimum effectiveness. Such a plan will reflect not only the best times for selling to the end user but also the ideal time to sell into distributors and retailers.

POSITION ANALYSIS

This is the 'where are we now?' stage of planning. We need to establish where our brand stands in each relevant country, market and sector at the time of preparing the plan.

In looking at any aspect of the campaign we must always be aware of the overall brand positioning; this is the glue which will hold integration together. However, individual campaigns – even for a single brand – will each have a specific job to do. Each must have its own clear objectives.

The specific campaign objectives must be developed from the relevant marketing and business objectives if the campaigns are to contribute to the bottom line. They must reflect the brand's unique positions in different sectors and geographic markets. A company or brand might be well established in its domestic market but be unknown in others. Communication activity needs to be sensitive to those circumstances. Competition will vary in the same way; a competitor might be powerful in Europe but weak in the Asia Pacific region.

A business objective might be to increase sales of Rover 800 series cars by 12 per cent in the next financial year. In such a sophisticated company, that objective itself would be supported by a defined strategy, to be delivered through the marketing objectives. The strategy would specify how many of each model are likely to make up the total, which markets they would be sold in and whether there is any seasonality in the marketplace.

The communication specialist needs to look at each of the target markets and the brand's local position. Rover is a serious player in the UK market – their communication is likely to be about establishing model preference while holding the premium image of the brand. In a country such as Japan, where Rover is perhaps less well known, the task may be to establish a premium positioning for the brand. We need to be clear on where our brand or brands stand in each sector or market. And we need to understand the competitive environment in those areas.

With that knowledge we can identify whether we are in the position of new entrant, niche holder or major player. We can say whether we are aggressively chasing more market share or defending our existing share. And we know whether we are seeking repeat purchase or new trial. In other words, we can begin to understand the role which communication must fulfil if we are to meet the business objective. That role is the basis for the communication objective.

However, to be as effective as possible in doing our job, we need to go further. We need to know what it is that makes our competitors successful in those markets. We must understand their positioning in the minds of customers and what value their brand or brands offer. This may well involve researching those brands with the same rigour we should apply to understanding our own.

COMMUNICATION OBJECTIVES

All communication seeks to persuade people to think, feel or act in a particular way in their relationship with a brand. Our objectives should, logically, be stated in those terms. And, just as is the case with business and marketing objectives, they should be quantified and time limited. They must display all of these characteristics of true objectives if we are to be able to measure our performance later.

The stages of the relationship between consumer and brand, and the steps taken to arrive at a purchase decision have been mapped in various ways over the years. Yet despite the efforts of many great minds, we still understand these things at little more than a superficial level. The combination of emotional and rational elements in a buying decision, combined with extensive external pressures mean that any purchase decision is very complex – and that each is probably unique.

Nevertheless, the majority of commentators believe that several basic steps in attitude change can be identified. Figure 4.2 shows the DAGMAR model developed by R H Colley in the early 1960s. It serves as a good example of what are generally agreed to be the main elements.

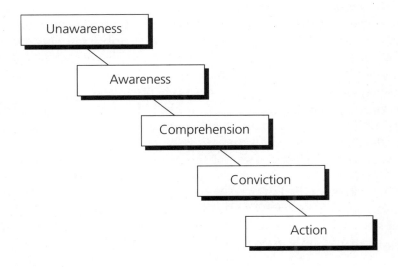

Figure 4.2 *The DAGMAR model*

Colley argues that consumers start by not knowing the brand, hence *unawareness*. They learn of its existence – *awareness* – then gradually develop an understanding of what the brand offers – the stage of *comprehension*. They come to believe the brand's message – *conviction* – and, finally, that the brand is right for them and so they buy – *action*.

We can usefully apply this model to our own market situations in order to help us identify what we want communication to do for the brand in each specific market.

Using the notional Rover example used earlier, this might lead to an objective in the UK market worded along the lines of 'to ensure that X per cent of the target audience score the Rover 600 series higher than any competitive model on the following criteria: . . .'. In the Japanese market the objective might be wider, for example 'to have X per cent of the target market identify the Rover 200 as one of their top five models in the prestige category for this size of car'.

Neither of these objectives is directly sales related but recognises the limitations of the communications process in selling cars, and the part which it can play in moving the potential customer closer to the purchase. Both respect the crucial nature of consumer attitude in determining success, and are developed from the point of view of influencing that attitude.

If we accept these basic steps towards a sale, we can identify a number of jobs which communication may legitimately be asked to do. We start by taking a particular part of our target market – as we did using the Japanese market for Rover. We need then to assess at which stage that market is currently. Inevitably this is a generalisation which will not hold true for every individual in our target group. However, in any mass market such generalisations are unavoidable. We can then assign communication's role.

Figure 4.3 illustrates some of the more common roles played by communication at each of the stages given in the DAGMAR model.

The history of the UK market for mobile telephones is an interesting example to use in discussing these various options. Cellular telephony was launched in Britain in January 1985. Prior to this date, most of us had only ever seen the concept in Dan Dare comic books or on Star Trek. The structure of the market was relatively complex because of governmental restrictions on the network owners, who were forbidden to sell 'air time' – another alien concept – directly to users. At the same time, neither the network owners nor their air time distributors were manufacturers of the actual telephones.

DAGMAR stage	Role for communication
Unawareness	To establish awareness of the brand's existence on the market.
Awareness	To increase the level of that awareness amongst a larger proportion of the target audience.
Comprehension	To educate or inform the audience about particular aspects of the brand.
Conviction	To establish particular perceptions or to correct mis-perceptions of the brand.
Action	To generate retailer visits, or mail/telephone responses. To prompt trial or sell products.

Figure 4.3 *Possible roles for communication*

The first task for all concerned was to make the market aware that the service was available. They started by targeting the business market. The immense level of press coverage given helped a great deal in achieving this. However, even those who knew of the service had little idea of what it offered or how it worked; there was an immense educational task to be done.

When the market began to pick up, mobile phones were regarded as being for either the chief executive or the 'flash Harry'. If mass sales were to be achieved, this perception had to be changed significantly.

Communication had, at the same time, a major task to fulfil in establishing preference between the two competing networks and amongst the numerous distributors. In parallel, at a more tactical level, much effort was being expended to generate enquiries for follow-up by the various sales forces.

With the business market well established, attention turned to the wider consumer market and the process more or less started again.

The relatively recent shift in distribution from specialists to High Street outlets, and the entry of new competitors such as the Orange brand from Hutchison Telecom have increased competition and the market has become more sales promotion led. Objectives now tend to be more aimed at trial and sale, although the Orange campaigns still aim to build major brand values.

In any dynamic market such as this, objectives may need to change fairly frequently to reflect the realities out in the marketplace. But the changes must be driven by shifts in the consumers' views of the market, not by the suppliers' needs. This particular case is fascinating in the way that objectives have moved back and forward across the theoretical model; witness, for example, the current backlash against the use of mobile phones in public places – marketers are having to readdress major attitudinal issues.

When we look at each part of our market from the customer's viewpoint, we can identify more easily what it is that our communication needs to do. Going through the exercise will also confirm whether we are indeed looking at one individual campaign or whether we need to segment our communication even further in order to address our market in the most meaningful way.

The final element of the objective is the message to be delivered: the campaign proposition. Arriving at this uses a similar process to that covered in Chapter 2. Our aim is to find a proposition which capitalises on what our brand has to offer, using an aspect of that offer which is important to our target market and which differs from the propositions used by our competitors. To help we can use a variant of Figure 2.2, shown here as Figure 4.4. We map competitors' positions relative to the main motivators in the market, marking them using circles whose size reflects market share. The resulting picture helps us identify the availability of a particular brand positioning on which to base the campaign proposition. In the larger market, for example, Heineken would be tucked well into the corner entitled 'refreshment'. It would be a long and tough battle to wrest that position from the brand – and probably not worth the effort in terms of the return achieved.

In the notional example shown, motivator A seems to be readily available; no brand dominates it and the nearest to it is not one of the biggest shareholders in the market. Motivator C may also be available since the big player in that segment does not seem to have fully convinced the market. How does our brand stack up against these two criteria? As stated in Chapter 2 under 'Towards a positioning', we are aiming to match what we have to offer against what is really important to our market.

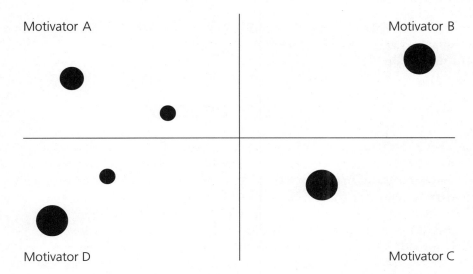

Figure 4.4 *Relative positioning strengths of competitors*

Inevitably, the process looks straightforward when distilled to its essence in this simplified form. In fact it takes insight and a generous helping of intellectual rigour to sift through the complex combination of emotional and rational elements in a market's views to arrive first at an understanding of what matters, then to identify where we should fit our brand.

The step from positioning to proposition relates to the point made at the beginning of this chapter: that each campaign has its specific objectives. A good example of this is some of the recent work for Kellogg's Cornflakes. The positioning as 'the sunshine breakfast cereal' has not changed but campaigns have been run both to extend usage and to recover lapsed users. These had specific objectives and – reading them as an outsider – specific propositions.

The campaign to extend usage retained the 'sunshine' feeling but sought to persuade the market that the cereal was an appropriate meal or snack at any time of the day. The proposition may have read something like: 'with Kellogg's Cornflakes you can have the sunshine feeling at any time'. The recovery campaign may have stemmed from 'do you remember how much you used to enjoy the sunshine feeling?'.

When we have written the proposition, we can write down the full objective in terms of audience feeling and reaction to the brand – and, for example, fill in the list of criteria referred to in the Rover case given earlier.

When we have defined and quantified the communication objectives, we are in a position to develop the strategy which will achieve them.

STRATEGY OPTIONS

There is a whole panoply of communication techniques available for our use in addressing any particular audience. Figure 4.5 lists just some of them and shows the vast range of media through which they can be applied. Neither list is exhaustive; they do however serve to indicate the extent of the options at our disposal when setting out to reach any particular audience. The advent of electronic media is already extending the list significantly. The presence of a PC on most office desks, for example, has opened up new possibilities in developing direct mail on computer disk. The growth in multimedia systems makes interactive CD-ROM disks a viable option in some markets. And of course we have the Internet, teletext, shopping channels and numerous other developments to be aware of.

Communication Techniques	Available Media
Face to face selling	National TV
Telephone and mail contact	Regional TV
Seminars	QTV
Exhibitions	Posters
Corporate identity	Bus sides/backs
Product design	Taxi media
Packaging design	National press
Point-of-sale materials	Regional press
Public relations	Special interest magazines
Media relations	Trade magazines
Advertising	Cinema
Direct mail	Radio
Sponsorship	Mail
Sales promotion	Door-to-door distribution
Member-get-member schemes	

Figure 4.5 *Communication techniques and available media*

Few campaigns use all of the tools of communication. Particular techniques are selected for their ability to do a particular job or aspect of the total job. One feature which almost all campaigns have in common is that they are based on a 'lead' activity such as advertising, and supported by a limited range of others. The aim is always the same: to get our message to the identified market as cost-effectively as we can.

Each of the available communications techniques has its own set of attributes which make it more suited to some tasks than others. Figure 4.6, developed by the Chartered Institute of Marketing for use in its diploma course, attempts to match techniques to a view of the stages of a purchase decision. The 'continuum of behaviour' used in the model shares many of the elements of the DAGMAR model shown earlier. However, although these indicators reflect the most common uses of the various tools, this is neither an exact nor a static science.

Each technique can be applied at almost any stage with some degree of success. And the 'rules' are broken frequently. Fifteen years ago, conventional wisdom said there was a – relatively low – limit to the value of goods which could be sold using direct marketing techniques. Today, products with price tickets running into literally thousands of pounds are successfully sold this way. Just ask Michael

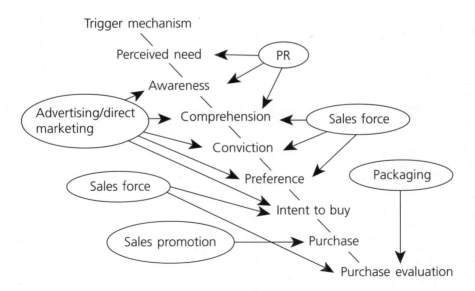

Figure 4.6 *Application of promotional tools*
(Chartered Institute of Marketing)

Dell, who has built a computer empire by selling direct. In the same way, advertising on bus backs was believed to be pointless if response generation was a key objective, yet this has been exposed as a fallacy in the telecommunications market.

The applicability of certain techniques does vary from market to market, and its success is not consistent across campaigns. There are many factors which influence overall results. As such, the following chapters can never be more than a guideline to help narrow down the options.

5

Advertising

It is appropriate to start with advertising since this is the option most frequently chosen to lead campaigns.

Advertising could be defined as the delivery of a message through space which is paid for by the advertiser. As consumers we are bombarded with many forms of advertising from television and radio commercials through newspaper and magazine advertisements to posters. It is a highly intrusive form of communication which – in one form or another – reaches every stratum and member of society. Its use varies from tiny classified ads to multi-page colour spreads in major national press, from studio-produced cinema commercials for the local garage to big-budget campaigns on national television. Using advertising can cost from a few pounds to many millions.

Advertising can help achieve almost any communication objective. It is a powerful tool for building awareness. If enough money is available, it can do so in a remarkably short time. The 'Tell Sid' campaign for the privatisation of British Gas, and the launch of the National Lottery both created high levels of awareness very quickly indeed (although we must bear in mind the high level of editorial coverage of both launches, which undoubtedly contributed to the total achievement).

Advertising can educate and inform. A simple application in the former case is the advertising used to announce a product recall! The campaigns run by the Central Office for Information on subjects such as drink driving and smoking fall into this category. It can certainly persuade, build reputation, condition preference and reassure those who have purchased; we are much more aware of advertising for a given product after we have bought it.

In the case of advertising used for direct marketing purposes, it even becomes the sales person. It can be persuasive enough to prompt prospects to buy products without sight or trial.

ADVERTISING – THE STRENGTHS AND WEAKNESSES

Strengths

Advertising can be both powerful and versatile. It lends itself to a wide variety of creative executions, which can be implemented using sight, sound and even – using 'scratch and sniff' technology – smell. And it's only a matter of time before we will be able to taste some products actually on the ads. It can be used for any type of product or service, although in a number of sectors such as tobacco products, its use is restricted by regulation or statute.

Subject to the particular medium used, advertising can also deal with complex messages and propositions. It has been widely used to explain fairly complicated arguments on behalf of specialist interest groups – witness the current battle over fox hunting. The whole issue of townification of rural lifestyles is highly complex. Yet advertising is tackling a number of aspects of the argument.

Perhaps the major strength of advertising lies in the fact that it is paid-for publicity. That means we can choose precisely the right media to reach our target audience, run the campaign when we choose and, most importantly, deliver the message in precisely the way we want – subject always to that message being 'legal, decent, honest and truthful'.

Weaknesses

The technique is not all-powerful. It acts as the sales person only in direct marketing; in the vast majority of situations it can only contribute to getting closer to the sale, usually by building the brand. And it can be difficult to pin down the precise contribution which it is making – unsurprising since our understanding of the process to the sale is imperfect.

The issue of measurement is important in considering advertising. Its effectiveness can be measured, but rarely totally. Even when using complex econometric models of a market's dynamics, it is almost impossible to be completely confident of an accurate measurement of success. However, if investment is made in the appropriate research, we can obtain a good idea of how well advertising is working.

Some audiences are difficult to reach cost-effectively with advertising. To use an extreme case, a manufacturer of particular pharmaceutical ingredients has less than 100 prospective customers in the whole of Europe. The right individuals within those organisations can be reached by specialist trade magazines but effective coverage of the audience would dictate the use of several magazines in a number of languages. In relative terms, advertising would be extremely expensive. Similarly, some audiences become caught in a curious middle ground. There are occasions when we are targeting consumers interested in a particular area, for example woodworking. Specialist magazines reach the real enthusiast but not the total audience. Conversely, national press can reach the whole audience but only at the expense of advertising to the great many readers who are not part of the target audience. Such 'wastage' can call into question the viability of using advertising.

This question of coverage of the audience goes hand in hand with the issue of how often we need to reach that audience, and in what timescale. These add up to the concept of 'threshold': the minimum amount of advertising which we can meaningfully run. There is little point in developing a TV campaign and only running the commercial once or twice. There are two reasons why: so few broadcasts are unlikely to have any lasting impact on the audience, and the production cost would make the price per consumer contact very high.

The weakness therefore is that, for any given situation, there is a minimum budget for advertising; this may mean excluding it from smaller campaigns.

Advertising's biggest weakness stems from human nature. We know we are being sold to, therefore we tend to view advertising with a healthy scepticism. The major creative challenge facing the advertiser or its agency is to overcome that scepticism with a credible proposition which motivates the audience.

THE SCOPE OF ADVERTISING

One thing advertising certainly offers is a variety of routes to reaching the audience. The following covers most of the options:

Television

Television can be used as either a national or a regional medium. It is flexible in terms of the types of package which can be bought: from individual time spots, to deals which guarantee to deliver a specified coverage of a defined audience. It is worth noting that using regional TV can give the feel of a big, national campaign to a local audience.

We can also use cable and satellite channels, many of which cover particular interest groups – the sports channel for example.

Cinema

Local advertisers can use particular cinemas, national advertisers can 'buy' coverage of a specific audience and, where context and relevance are important, the advertiser can book to 'follow the film' – when the commercial will move around with a particular movie. Like TV, cinema offers all the options of visuals, sound and movement.

Radio

Radio is available as a local, regional or national medium and, with the advent of so many new channels in the 1980s and 1990s, radio offers lots of scope for advertising to people with a particular interest or lifestyle. Radio offers an interesting creative challenge in that we have to invite the listener to create the picture. It can be highly cost-effective for just this reason. There is no other medium where we could create an intergalactic war for a few hundred pounds.

The disadvantage is perhaps that radio tends to be 'wallpaper'. We are inclined to listen to it while doing something else. Therefore, advertising on radio demands frequent repetition to create effective message transmission and a lasting result.

Newspapers

Local, regional and national press are all available although in the first two the quality of publication varies a great deal as does the amount of real readership they attract. Some 'local' newspapers such as *The Yorkshire Post* or *The Glasgow Herald* have as much stature in their constituencies as do national papers.

Newspapers allow us to deliver longer and more complex messages than can usually be sent by TV, cinema or radio. The reader spends more time with them and , generally, is prepared to absorb more detail.

Magazines

The variety available is staggering. There is a wide range of general interest publications, from the frothiness of *Hello* to the weightiness of *The New Statesman*. Special interest magazines abound, from the half-dozen game fishing magazines to which I fall victim every month, to knitting, music, bee keeping, DIY and many other subject areas. Every profession has its own publications addressing relevant business and technical issues.

One particular feature of magazines is that they are a 'personal' medium. We are exposed to them on a one-to-one basis. This can be important to the advertiser. The UK campaign for Häagen Dazs ice cream used women's mags for precisely that reason. Self-indulgence was the message, and that is not something you share with others, hence the personal nature of magazines was ideal for carrying the advertising.

Outdoor advertising

This all-encompassing term covers a lot of ground. Those big '48-sheet' posters are the most conspicuous version of outdoor advertising. They are powerful and eye-catching, but they are far from the only option.

Bus sides, bus backs and taxi sides can all offer mobile billboards. Bus stop 'adshel' posters, 'tube cards' on underground trains, and 'cross-track' posters at railway stations and in tube stations can all reach consumers on the move. And this latter group can carry relatively long messages since the audience is 'captive' during the waiting period – and has little to do except read the posters.

If you have attended any sports venue, you will have seen posters around the running track, football pitch or horse-race track. And of course every shopper is exposed to point-of-sale material, which varies from 'outdoor' – as window posters, to 'indoor' – as shelf stickers and so on.

Other options

Even the above list does not cover all the options. Others include the Internet, QTV, a service offered by the Post Office which has screens in each post office, running commercials, and on-video advertising where commercials are built into rental videos in an effort to exploit a large and growing market. We have seen advertising carried on everything from the sides of cows (by a farmer in the USA) to milk bottles!

One of the most important media for many companies is their own transport. Trucks and vans are no more or less than mobile showcases for a company message and can be used very effectively as such.

6

Public Relations

Public relations is a much misunderstood discipline. There may have been a time when the field was occupied by the 'gin and tonic brigade'. To rest in the belief that this remains the case is to dismiss out of hand one of the most powerful communication techniques at our disposal.

For too many companies, PR amounts to producing the occasional press release, probably written in-house by someone who is expert in neither PR nor in creative writing!

Inevitably, PR uses many of the same media as advertising, but uses them in different ways and with different objectives. To understand these differences it is important to have a sound grasp of the purposes to which public relations can be put.

CORPORATE APPLICATIONS OF PR

Most large companies are publicly owned. The state of their share prices significantly affects their ability and freedom to manage the future. An undervalued company cannot, for example, borrow as freely as one which is fairly valued. Yet share prices are not set by absolute measures but rather by the opinions of relatively few stock analysts and major investors. Their perception of the business is all-important. PR is a crucial weapon in ensuring that they see the company in a fair light. It is a key tool in managing the relationship between the company and these people who can have such a profound effect on its future.

We live in a legislative society and that legislation can make or break even major corporations. In UK terms, a change of government from Conservative to Labour or vice versa will make an enormous difference in the political and economic environment in which the company must operate. The single issue of nationalisation – or indeed denationalisation – can close or open huge markets in the space of months. At European level, the introduction of the Euro has pushed business leaders into taking a stance one way or the other. Good strategic use of public relations can help ensure that the company's voice is heard to good effect in the relevant corridors of power – before precipitate decisions are taken. In this way, the company's opinion can be put before officials, members of parliament, ministers, leaders of pressure groups or trade unions, thus optimising the chance of decisions being made in the light of a sound analysis of all of the evidence.

PR can deliver this kind of help across a whole range of areas including community relations, environmental issues, financial relations, consumer affairs, issues management and crisis handling.

This last area is often forgotten until it is too late. When the disaster has happened is not the time to start considering the options. The damage is done. Any manufacturing business, for example, is at risk of accidents in the workplace. Most will have defined safety policies and all should of course do everything possible to reduce the potential for any such event. However, each should also have a strategy in place to deal with the eventuality. Who should be notified? How? Who is authorised to speak to the press? How will the response statement be prepared? By whom?

Corporate public relations encompasses the preparation for such situations and many others. It can play a central role at corporate level. As an aside, it is also worth noting that – when this value is understood within the company – public relations can provide the practitioner with regular and close access to the highest echelons in the company!

BRAND PR

Closer to what we might describe as more customer-associated PR, the discipline can make a real difference in our efforts to position the brand, whether product or corporate. If we seek to be seen as an innovative company, for example, a regular flow of information on new developments or research can give a substantive boost to the customer perception we are trying to create. Similarly, a series of media-attractive events of the appropriate type can build the product brand positioning.

Brand PR is often based on press relations rather than 'public relations' in the fullest sense. It can vary from the simple issuing of a press release, to a full strategic programme aimed at establishing relationships with particular journalists, businesses, commentators or trend-setters in the particular marketplace. The key to success lies in understanding the interests and needs of the particular sector of the media we wish to target; in other words, we treat them like any other target audience which is important to us.

Specific tactics vary from regular briefings – such as quarterly press lunches or seminars of some form – through submitting products to test panels, something which can be very effective in the computer market, to placed features written in the editorial style of a target publication and with publication agreed in advance.

THE NATURE OF 'NEWS'

Publications will only print material which they perceive to have real value to their readers, thus enhancing the standing of their own brand, the publication. It stands to reason therefore that we must produce material which responds to that reality. The need to tailor and package our messages appropriately is paramount.

A national daily newspaper is looking for 'hot' items – yesterday's news is no news. The Sunday papers want the same, but with a more in-depth treatment. The 'quality papers' will give news a different treatment to the tabloids such as the *Sun*. Monthly magazines, trade publications, specialist interest magazines – all have different editorial needs and platforms. Is it any wonder that blanket press releases have such limited success unless the news issued is genuinely earth-shattering?

Few companies can keep up a regular flow of genuine news but that does not mean that they cannot create news. Events can be created around newsworthy happenings elsewhere. Nike could capitalise on the London Marathon. Airlines cash in on the Olympics by running features and special flights around the period. Research can be used to generate news. It is not difficult to imagine a shoe manufacturer researching how much walking the average Briton does each day – and getting headlines like 'Britain gets lazy'.

STRENGTHS OF PR

PR is very flexible, perhaps even more so than advertising. It can respond very quickly to events as they unfold, providing that the strategy to do so is in place in advance. It has the power to give a direct and relatively short-term boost to corporate financial health. It can be applied to the benefit of all levels of the corporation or brand.

In press relations, the single greatest strength which PR can offer is credibility. In the same way that we tend to have a healthy scepticism of advertising, we – even today – tend to believe what we read in our favourite publications. Thus the independence of journalistic comment gives weight to our message.

PR objectives need to be derived from corporate and marketing objectives – and to be both realistic and definable. We must understand and agree what constitutes success.

Media relations campaigns, at their most effective, are driven by analysis and evaluation systems that can provide continuous data on the penetration of key messages and brand values. Such systems help keep the PR work tightly focused, whether managing a corporate issue in the business community, or benchmarking against competitors in the media.

Naturally, PR works best when integrated with all other activities. For example, it can help create a positive media environment in which advertising can run.

WEAKNESSES OF PR

The major weakness of PR activity is lack of controllability. We can rarely guarantee when our message will be delivered – if at all. We are at the mercy of the recipient as to what will be done with our transmission. Therefore, in contrast with advertising, we cannot be sure of timing, coverage or message content – let alone tone of voice or interpretation.

These weaknesses can be countered to an extent by a well prepared strategic plan for PR, as described above, but they will never be fully overcome.

MEASURING SUCCESS

One of the most encouraging developments of recent years has been in more sophisticated systems for measuring the worth of a PR campaign.

Historically, counting column inches was about as far as most analysis went. However, enormous coverage of a negative nature would score highly in such a system but is most unlikely to be what we want to achieve.

Today's approach might measure column centimetres, number of brand mentions and the extent of accurate reproduction of the desired message. It might compare our scores with those of our major competitors. In this way, we begin to get a truer picture of the effect our efforts are having in the market.

7

Direct Mail to Relationship Marketing

Direct mail was the fastest growing communication technique right through the Eighties. Its appeal lies in the fact that it is the most easily measurable of all those techniques available to the marketer. We can 'count them out and count them back'. It is relatively simple to set up a system which records the total cost of mailing a given part of our target market. It is almost as easy to capture details of responses received and, using the kind of 'contact' software available today, to track those responses through to final sale. Thus we know, in terms of direct mail cost, exactly how much each sale has cost and can calculate the return on investment in a direct and meaningful way.

Unfortunately nothing in life is that simple. Nor is success guaranteed. A look at the strengths and weaknesses of the technique may give some insight into the potential problems.

STRENGTHS OF DIRECT MAIL

The ideal communication with a prospective customer takes place in a face-to-face meeting. The members of any agency creative team will tell you that the best advertising does not talk to 'markets', it talks to an individual. Direct mail is the 'mass-communication' technique which comes closest to allowing us to convey a personal message to the recipient.

By careful targeting and list selection, we can group prospects into sections of the population with common interests or attitudes and thus frame our message in a way which is more directly relevant to that smaller group. As we become increasingly skilled at segmenting our audiences in various ways, direct mail is becoming a more and more effective technique. And the degree of segmentation to which we go is limited only by the cost of producing different implementations of our base message.

Direct mail lets us segment as far as we wish and provides us with an efficient medium for delivery to the target segments.

It offers another significant advantage in allowing us, cost-effectively, to vary the elements within the message to find which appeal most to our market. A typical mailing might contain, say, a covering letter, a brochure, a special offer leaflet, a reply card or other response mechanisms and an envelope. In a large mailing such as *Reader's Digest* or the Automobile Association carry out regularly, the message alternatives can be tested on a relatively small sample of the total audience and proven before mass mailing is carried out. So, for example, we could test whether '50 per cent off' has more or less audience appeal than '2 for the price of 1'. Each element of the mailing can be tested individually, prior to making the final major investment.

This leads to the third significant benefit direct mail can offer: predictability. If the test sample is large enough for statistical confidence, we know – within defined mathematical limits – that the final mailing will give the same result as the test mailing. So we have validated our main investment at relatively low cost and risk.

WEAKNESSES OF DIRECT MAIL

There are practical problems in many markets. The quality of the lists which are available for rental is highly variable, and they might not offer the precise audience breakdown which we require. In an ideal mailing, we send our pack only to those who are likely to be highly interested in it; that's what will give the most cost-effective result. In reality, we will usually be faced with an element of wastage in any rented list which we use. (I will deal with our own in-house lists later.)

The main problems occur in trying to find lists giving precisely the audience definition we seek, and with lists which are not brought up to date frequently enough – in extreme cases, still supplying details of people long since dead.

In my own experience, the other weakness of direct mail is that it is not a powerful tool for building brands. By its nature, this is not a 'visible' medium – it does not create impact on a broad scale. This can cause short-term problems in markets where the company relies heavily on its channels of distribution; the promise of a direct mail campaign to support the brand simply does not motivate the distributors in the way in which a high-profile advertising campaign can. For major consumer brands, total reliance on direct mail would be an immense risk since the public persona of a brand – how others will perceive *me* as a user of the brand – is a key part of the marketing of that brand.

THE ROLE OF DIRECT MAIL

Direct mail has a large part to play for any company faced with relatively small audiences. It can be the only viable medium for regular contact.

It is also an excellent support technique to run behind, say, an advertising and PR campaign. It can carry very long and detailed messages – which will be read and absorbed if the targeting is right and the creative solution well designed.

Direct mail is an excellent route to generating response. As a nation, we are used to receiving it both in our business and personal lives. And despite all the 'junk mail' jibes, the vast majority of us 'clip the coupon' several times a year. If the proposition is right for the audience, the responses will come. For this reason, direct mail plays a central role in many business-to-business campaigns.

It can also be used, through a series of mailings, to divide a complex message into several elements and deliver them in 'bite-sized chunks'. This can be important when seeking to educate an audience or in dealing with difficult issues – AIDS, smoking and health, environmental issues and so on.

DATABASE MARKETING

Database marketing is essentially an extension of direct mail activity. Simply put, it involves capturing all corporate contacts and assembling them into a database which holds all information which we possess on each customer or prospect.

Most companies have an immense amount of information on their customers, at least on their direct customers. In our own businesses we will have details of what was bought, when and at what price. With decent software, it is not difficult to establish preferences for product types, and to identify ordering patterns from this information. Data presented in a manner which gives us visibility of such information is invaluable. We can use it to approach each individual or target company with a specifically targeted proposition which we already know will be of interest to them. We can also market more effectively to the converted; those customers trusted us once and, provided we gave good service before, are more likely than the average to trust us again.

To use a straightforward case, a music club which gains a response from a mailing of its general catalogue can identify from the responses those interested in, say, jazz. A follow-up mailing – perhaps sent as part of the delivery of the original order – could contain special offers on jazz-related products. This principle applies in most markets. A vendor of computer supplies could identify the types of computer a business uses from its early ordering patterns and content – and tailor subsequent offers to suit.

Our existing customers are our easiest targets, and a database in the right format and structure for easy marketing use is a superb tool to exploit that resource. In addition, the database allows us to develop detailed profiles of our customers. When we then seek lists for further mailings, we can use those profiles to identify our best prospects.

The value of such a database will become even more evident when we look at a more recent development, *relationship marketing*.

RELATIONSHIP MARKETING

In many markets, competitive pressure has risen so much that the cost of acquiring a new customer actually outweighs the immediate benefit accrued from the first sale. Even where this is not the case, acquisition costs are rising steadily in most markets, making customer retention of prime importance to the long-term health of the business. Marketers recognise that holding on to those valuable assets, their customers, means building a genuine relationship with the brand.

At one level, this means ensuring that the brand continues to deliver what the consumer expects, and indeed changes as consumer needs change. Thus we see the occasional repositioning of brands.

At a practical level, managing the relationship means finding ways of keeping the customer loyal to the brand and the products or services which it represents. Hence the birth of relationship marketing and the many loyalty schemes we see – and probably participate in – today.

The 'Association' Model

Interestingly, although this is thought of as a new development, the roots of this model were laid down decades ago. Cooperatives could well be described as loyalty schemes (with co-ownership as a bonus). Certainly various interest groups, associations and professional bodies have been 'relationship marketing' for many years.

The Chartered Institute of Marketing, with which I am personally involved, is a typical example. It strives to raise standards and profile within the profession. However, to do this it must retain its membership. It aims to do so by giving membership a high profile and supports this central aim with access to local branch meetings, discounted deals on training, special rates negotiated with a wide range of suppliers in car hire, hotels and so on.

The feeling of 'belonging to an exclusive club' is central to the relationship between a professional body and its members. That belonging is core to successful relationship marketing.

The commercial version

Much of what is happening in business is built on similar foundations. The implementation can range from a magazine to much more integrated and complex benefit packages.

The magazine, published under contract, is a growing phenomenon. The Automobile Association magazine has a circulation of several millions to its members. British Airways' *High Life* magazine, published for the company, is reputed to generate profits in its own right – surely the ultimate achievement. Every airline carries its own magazine, most supermarket chains have their own, the credit card companies and many other financial institutions are avid proponents of the medium.

We might indulge in a chicken and egg argument at this point. Which came first, the programme or the database? Like the classic question, there is no meaningful answer! If we don't have a means of capturing customer information in a meaningful and usable way, there's no need for a database. If we don't have a database, the information gathering is pointless. Both are essential for success.

Microsoft is a good case in point. The company has many millions of users, but they do not buy direct so the brand owner has little opportunity to influence loyalty. Microsoft in the UK set out to attack this issue by getting its internal act together. It restructured and refined its database system, built a programme to increase the percentage of registration cards returned by consumers direct to the company, and started managing its relationships.

Today it can target relatively small segments of its customer base according to a range of criteria. It offers particular support packages. It sells more product, and it does so cost-effectively. Among its keener users it is creating that sense of belonging through these activities and with regular, tailored communications.

A call for help

A particularly personal and visible manifestation of this trend is customer helplines. We expect to find these in markets such as computers – where we can readily see the need for help cropping up. However, they are by no means restricted to technical products or services. Boots, the chemist chain set up a line for customers who suffered from hay fever. It offered a reliable, up-to-date pollen count. In 12 weeks over 100,000 calls were taken. Although providing an altruistic service – no selling was involved – the company gained valuable information about its customer base. Have you used the Persil care line to find out more about the brand's many variants? Thousands have. Just as many Burger King customers have passed comment over the chain's 0800 free call line.

The willingness of consumers to make use of such services should not be underestimated: Microsoft takes a million calls a year. That's a million opportunities to create a delighted customer, opportunities which would otherwise be lost to the brand.

The sell can of course be much harder as relationship marketing begins to combine with sales promotion. Witness the success of Air Miles in building a loyal following.

THE SIGNIFICANCE OF RELATIONSHIP MARKETING

Market share is increasingly hard to win from competitors. Yet all of us suffer some level of regular attrition in our customer base (known as the churn rate in the mobile phones business). If we could halve the level of attrition, the effect on the bottom line would be significant. This makes relationship marketing not only a financially viable, but a highly desirable strategic option.

8

Sponsorship

Sponsorship continues to suffer from two misconceptions which we can correct immediately. It is not a donation given to create a warm corporate feeling, and it is not a cynical exploitation of a sporting, artistic or other event. It is simply another tool in our armoury of communication weapons. Used properly, it can help meet corporate or brand objectives – and at the same time support worthwhile causes in the community.

Sponsorship can and indeed should be carefully targeted. It can be used strategically or tactically. And its performance can be measured to at least the same extent as advertising performance.

However, like all of our weapons, it has limitations. It rarely works effectively on its own. Its strengths and weaknesses both stem from its basic character. It is a relatively passive form of communication. In many instances we achieve only exposure of the brand name. Therefore we are leaving it to the audience to do most of the work in defining the message which we are trying to send, and in decoding it for themselves. This can be powerful in a sophisticated market where the consumer is likely to have a level of resistance to a harder sell. It does mean, however, that our choice of what to sponsor is absolutely critical if the target effect is to be achieved.

Sponsorship is most emphatically not a 'chuck and chance it' option. It demands the same analytical approach which we apply to the use of any communication technique. And, as always, the start point is what we want to get out of the investment: our communication objective.

SPONSORSHIP OBJECTIVES

Sponsorship has the capacity to deliver in a number of areas of communication. The right package can create or reinforce high name awareness. This particularly true when television coverage can be achieved as part of the package. The Embassy Snooker Tournament certainly was very effective in the tobacco sector, where advertising opportunities are limited. However, we should bear in mind that name awareness in itself will rarely achieve our total objectives – unless we achieve product or brand association through that awareness, it has little effective purpose. Where such activity is at its strongest is in supporting other communication techniques to deliver brand awareness, product understanding and purchase preference.

Sponsorship of the right event offers excellent opportunities for customer and staff entertaining. A day at the races – or equivalent – can prove a valuable catalyst for relationship building or for employee motivation.

Supporting the local community can make a great difference to how a company is viewed by its neighbours. It can also help show the business in a favourable light and thus make recruitment easier.

When sponsorship gives access to well-known individuals, personal appearances can be used to attract target visitors to the sponsor's premises – for a seminar for example.

The point is that we must know what we want from sponsorship before even starting the planning process.

PLANNING SPONSORSHIP

Figure 8.1 shows the process of planning sponsorship activity. The key lies, once again, in our understanding of the target audience which we wish to influence. We must know what they are like – their innate characteristics – and what, therefore, they are likely to be interested in.

A lifestyle profile of the audience will reveal those areas of particular interest to them, whether sporting, musical, related to different hobbies or whatever. It is these areas – where our targets' interests are higher than the norm – that we expect to find the most effective sponsorship opportunities. It is this stage of the analysis at which we begin to form a view of the strategic approach we will use. Carling, the brewers, would have found at this point that a high proportion of beer drinkers are interested in sports, therefore they

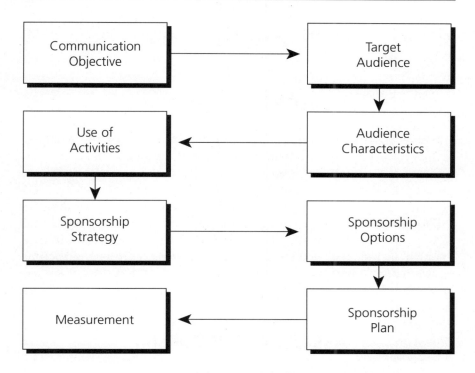

Figure 8.1 *Planning sponsorship activities*

would have compiled a list of possible sponsorship opportunities in that specific field.

Further analysis and a narrowing of 'sports' down to those most popular with the audience led them to soccer. A close look at what could be done led them eventually to a sponsorship plan led by a deal with the Football League.

As those options were narrowed, Carling would have looked from the audience's viewpoint to find an option which was consistent with the values of the brand. And that's the key measure of a sponsorship choice: does it reflect values which complement those of the brand itself? To give an example, if Garrards the royal jewellers found that a high proportion of their customers were darts fans, they would still be unlikely to sponsor the sport because its image would not reflect theirs. Polo or horse racing would, however, appear to be viable options.

Sponsorship options are increasing, particularly in the relaxation of the rules on sponsorship of TV programmes. The insurance group Legal & General exploited this by sponsoring the weather forecasts: a nice example of straight product association at work. The fact that their logo is an umbrella makes the sponsorship choice even more apt.

SPONSORING INDIVIDUALS

Another pertinent example was the use by Pepsi of the Michael Jackson concerts. But this also highlighted the problem of an alliance with an individual. Jackson was singularly appropriate to take a message to Pepsi's target audience. However, when he was accused of a string of offences against young children, the value of their $5 million investment fell with a resounding bump. Jackson never came to trial, yet there almost certainly was damage to the brand in any event. This risk also applies in sponsoring, for example, a particular sports team. When 'your' team gets relegated, what does it do for your brand's image?

AREAS OF SPONSORSHIP

Television offers name and logo mentions around specific pro-grammes. The UK is a long way behind the USA in this respect, where a much more pervasive presence on the part of the sponsor is the norm. Radio also offers similar, indeed wider, opportunities.

Sporting events are usually the first thing to come to mind when the word sponsorship is mentioned. This is for a good reason. Sports are telegenic so there is a good chance of achieving some TV cover-age during the sponsorship period. The rules on sponsorship are flexible: for example, football teams invariably carry a sponsor's name prominently on their shirts these days. And of course, most people are interested in some form of sporting activity – if only as couch potatoes!

However, the popularity of sports sponsorships means that good opportunities can be both expensive and hard to come by.

The arts are also heavily sponsored and in many ways, from individual events to annual competitions for young musicians and so on. Music has almost universal appeal and, in one form or another, is capable of helping the sponsor reach virtually any audience.

Community sponsorship can take many forms– from making a donation to the local boy scout troop, to donating a new library to the town. They can range through restoration of the local canal to underwriting the cost of 'bottle banks' or street furniture such as waste bins.

Publications will often accept deals on special supplements or competitions – where sponsorship overlaps with sales promotion.

Many professional organisations run annual conferences for which they seek support. These can be a useful way to reach specific interest groups and business audiences.

If no suitable sponsorship opportunity exists, you can create one. One mortgage lender sponsors an annual award for the estate agent of the year – an award which was created specifically for the company.

COMMUNICATING THE SPONSORSHIP

Specialists have a simple rule of thumb. For every pound sterling you propose to invest in sponsorship, you should have another one ready to invest in exploiting the sponsorship.

The Pepsi case mentioned earlier is a prime example. Michael Jackson was used extensively in their advertising during the term of the agreement. Special offer cans, competitions and other events were all spun off the core package. The mortgage company puts great effort into media relations to ensure that the competition gets covered by the key trade press and the national press, and that the winners receive plenty of publicity.

There is little point in investing in sponsorship unless we set out to optimise the benefits of that investment. Spending several million pounds supporting a round-the-world yacht race is fairly pointless unless we ensure our target markets recognise the sponsorship. Part of our planning must be looking at how we leverage the activity to best effect using all of the communication techniques at our disposal.

9

Design

The influence of design is all-pervasive. It stretches from the name and identity of the brand, through the physical properties of the product all the way to whether our press release paper will help draw the attention of an editor. Design is a central element of communication yet many companies, particularly industrial companies, leave it entirely to engineers rather than marketers – and often don't think of it at all in terms of communication.

The appearance of a product, its packaging, its advertising, all have a part to play in creating an emotive response from a customer or potential customer. That response is the core of everything we seek to achieve in communication – and indeed in the full spectrum of marketing. Design should therefore be given a great deal of attention by the communication specialist and by many others in the business.

Let's take a look at what design can do for the brand. We will examine this under four headings:

1. the products themselves;
2. the brand identity;
3. the packaging; and
4. the specific attributes which apply to publicity activity.

PRODUCT DESIGN

'If it looks right, it probably is right' is an old engineering adage – but a perceptive one. We all react to the physical appearance of any product. At one extreme is our reaction to fashion goods where appearance is almost everything; all other purchase considerations are secondary. In this context, finding the right 'label' on a clothing item would qualify as part of its physical characteristics.

Perhaps surprisingly we find the same reaction, albeit to a lesser degree, in markets such as capital goods. I have seen restyling exercises on commercial vehicles move popular perception from 'a bit old fashioned' to 'right up to date' – and have watched sales respond accordingly. The 'product' had not changed in so far as it was the same truck with the same features and the same perform- ance. The restyling was purely cosmetic. You didn't really think business purchases were totally rational did you?

Physical design communicates a great deal about the product and hence the brand. Tango's bright orange may be literally appropriate for an orange drink, but it's also singularly apt for a fresh, bright, fun brand. Somehow it is difficult to imagine the same colour rein- forcing Volvo's positioning around 'safety'.

Swatch watches have transformed product design into an art form. They are their own positioning, packaging and promotion all rolled up into one. Interestingly, as a non-expert, I suspect they only make one watch movement. The rest could be described as packa- ging. And extremely successful it is, too.

Colour, weight, style and shape all send subconscious messages. See a certain shape of bottle, with absolutely no markings and most consumers would identify Coca Cola. Other shapes might say Mateus Rosé (at least to those of us who took it to every party in the 1960s), or Grolsch beer.

Physical design plays a big part in repeat purchases. A top which is difficult to remove could kill repeat business. A car seat which caused fatigue on long journeys would soon have the motoring press baying for blood.

BRAND OR CORPORATE IDENTITY

This is possibly the area of design which we associate most readily with the communication task. And it's easy to see why. Figure 9.1 shows the same fictional brand name in four standard typefaces. What impression does each create of the brand? Your own views may differ but to me the top left typeface suggests a delicate, femi- nine brand, and the top right, uncompromising solidity. The bottom left feels modern and clean-cut while the last one suggests tradition and trustworthiness.

Sondrex　　　**Sondrex**

Sondrex　　　**Sondrex**

Figure 9.1 *What do the different typefaces say about the brand?*

Of course, my notional brand name may itself have coloured your views. However, product naming is a whole book in itself and one would hope that by the time you get to planning communication that that has been well sorted out using research among key target groups.

Name and brand name design are obviously important in consumer goods but they can also influence sales of capital equipment. One Midlands company launched a robot-based labeller which was attacked by competitors as being too lightweight. Competitive equipment was several hundred pounds of metal – to apply a label weighing a few grams! The company launched a Mark II variant and named it *Bicepta*. This fairly logical development, from robotic arm to a name based on the main arm muscle, helped fight the competitive battle.

Corporate identity can also precondition prospects as to what to expect of a company. Logo and typography set the scene – even if subconsciously – before we meet the prospect. A messy, busy design will tend to betray a small company trying to look big. A confident, clean design which allows plenty of space in the design will look more like a company which has already made it. What is right for a firm of solicitors is almost certainly very wrong for a young dynamic software company.

PACKAGING DESIGN

Pack design in consumer products can make the difference between success and failure. It plays a major role in launching new products where the decision to buy is often made at the supermarket shelf. For products which depend on impulse purchase its role is paramount.

Today, considerations go much further than merely the outward look of the pack. Witness the growth of refill packs under the advance of more enlightened attitudes on the impact of packaging waste on the environment. The modern consumer, depending on his or her attitudes, will look for a whole series of satisfactions from the packaging associated with a particular brand.

Functionality is, of course, important: there's no incentive to buy a carton of milk brand if it goes all over the kitchen worktop when it's opened. 'Family' packs of products may need built-in handles so they can be carried home easily. Fail to provide them and the product positioning which you have worked out so carefully could be irreparably damaged in the eyes of the consumer. Protection is important for most products; even new trucks have a wax coating to prevent damage to the paintwork during transit.

For some audiences, pack design may need to go much further, taking into account the waste issue and recyclability. For sensitive consumers, the sheer amount of packaging material can be a turn-off. And which of us has not complained about the cost of packaging on a chocolate Easter egg?

It is worth noting that the effectiveness of packaging can be tested and measured fairly accurately using mock shops set up specifically for the purpose. A number of major research houses now offer this service from their own permanent facilities.

PUBLICITY DESIGN

Advertising always works better when it is conceived as a long-term campaign and based around a single, strong advertising idea. All forms of publicity work better when they show consistency of design, feel and tone of voice.

Some years ago a few of my colleagues asked me to write a case study of some work they had done for the computer manufacturer, Hewlett-Packard. Over almost three years they had progressively tested all the elements of the advertising and direct mail the agency was producing for the client. The two activities had been done separately for most of that period. A real breakthrough occurred when they adopted the same creative idea for both, and designed the elements in concert. Response to both the advertising and the direct mail rose by around 20 per cent.

The pack design must have empathy with images and design used in the publicity activity or we are in real danger of sending conflicting messages. We should make sure the literature complies with both. Indeed, every element which we use should have a common 'look'. We will come back to this subject as we look at implementing integrated communication.

10

Exhibitions, Conferences and Seminars

Most companies at some time or other take part in an exhibition or conference, or organise a seminar. It is perhaps worth starting this chapter by taking a look at the main characteristics of each format.

Essentially, an exhibition is a public event organised by an independent organisation and which can be attended by any business that meets the very broad parameters that are typically applied to such events. They can be designed to appeal to a broad audience – as with the annual *Ideal Home* exhibition – or for highly specific audiences – in the case of exhibitions such as PAKEX, aimed at packaging and packaging machinery users.

Conferences share many aspects with exhibitions, and indeed the two often run side by side. The major difference lies in the display facilities available at exhibitions; conferences are generally aimed at sharing knowledge through speeches without the addition of product displays. Thus exhibitions have a selling focus not normally shared by conferences.

In contrast, seminars are normally run as more private events, exclusive to the organising company and often held on company premises. By their nature, they are usually on a much smaller scale than either of the others – although some can easily rival major conferences in size and number of attendees.

COMPARATIVE SELLING POWER

Exhibitions, conferences and seminars are all very different selling environments. The conference is a 'soft sell'. It can be excellent for establishing the company as an expert voice in its industry but creates only limited opportunities for really selling. Exhibitions are perhaps the mid-point. They are good for making new contacts but as a true selling environment they are somewhat limited.

Seminars are different. The agenda is yours and the territory is yours. They can be first-rate opportunities to do real business.

The variations in the characteristics of each are important in assessing whether they have a role in any particular integrated communication campaign.

USING EXHIBITIONS

Matching the audience

Exhibition organisers will invest only in areas where they have forecast enough audience and exhibitor interest to give a reasonable prospect of a healthy return on that investment. No single exhibitor is likely to have a great deal of influence over whether an exhibition does or doesn't take place. So our only option is to use exhibitions which are already planned.

The first task is to identify whether there are any exhibitions aimed at our particular audience. The likelihood is that there will be; there is a plethora of exhibitions covering a vast range of target audiences and product fields.

In business and industrial marketing, there are exhibitions in the most esoteric of specialist areas. Consumer exhibitions are perhaps less common, particularly in fast moving consumer goods. However, if we include such events as companies displaying at, for example, the Radio 1 Roadshow, the horizons broaden (but this type of activity is closer to sponsorship and will not be covered here). Even though numerically less common, there are still many consumer exhibitions in areas such as home computing, travel, interior decoration, arts and crafts, sports and a whole panoply of hobby fields.

Why attend?

Simply, if you've chosen the right exhibition, many key prospective customers will attend. They will have given up valuable time to attend, and they will have a genuine interest in the subject. That makes them valuable contacts. Our objective in attending could be just that: to establish X new contacts within our target market.

Most exhibitions attract good media representation. If we have something fresh to say, perhaps a new product to launch, an exhibition can provide a high profile environment in which to launch it to both the media and the target audience.

A third valid reason for attending is during the early stages of entering a new market or region. The visibility gained can establish the company or brand as a 'player' in the particular market.

There are two frequently given reasons for attending exhibitions which, in my view, have no validity: 'we're going because our competitors are there', and 'if we don't go, we'll be missed and everyone will think we're in trouble'. Such negative reasons are guaranteed to waste money. Either exhibition attendance helps meet the business and communication objectives, or it doesn't. There is no other sensible measure of the value of taking part.

The sales opportunity

Daniel in the lions' den! That is certainly one view of exhibitions. We are stuck in the middle of all of our major competitors, fighting for the attention of the limited number of visitors; after all, even big exhibitions rarely attract as many visitors as would read a major daily newspaper. And at big events, they will not get around to visiting every exhibition.

Yet the competitors are in the same boat. It's neutral territory and the company that is best at managing exhibition attendance effectively will come out the winner. We'll return to this point under 'publicising our participation', later in this chapter.

CONFERENCE OPPORTUNITIES

While an exhibition can take on the hustle and bustle of the old bazaar in Cairo, the conference is more akin to the reverential atmosphere of the lecture theatre. The format is structured, with only limited time available for 'networking'. It is not generally conducive to selling in any real sense; not least because delegates don't expect to be sold to at such events and are therefore less predisposed and more resistant to approaches.

But conferences really come into their own in helping position the expertise inherent in a business brand. Regular appearances on the conference circuit can greatly enhance reputation – which can be crucial in business-to-business marketing.

Good conferences do get good coverage, particularly in specialist media, and can therefore add weight to the company's overall media relations effort.

If no speaking opportunity is available, it can be worth considering going to a conference as a delegate. However, we should attend with clear views of who else is likely to be there, and whom we want to make contact with. The skill is in 'working the crowd' to establish contact with important target individuals within our total audience. The achievable number of contacts will be much lower than at a major exhibition. This is inevitable in that conference delegate numbers only infrequently exceed several hundred, compared to the thousands we would expect at even a fairly small exhibition.

THE ROLE OF SEMINARS

Open days, customer days, seminars: a rose by any other name would smell as sweet! There are many descriptive terms but the principle is consistent. We seek to get a group of customers and prospects to a venue of our choosing in a captive situation so we can sell to them.

In many senses this is an ideal selling situation. The challenge lies in persuading the right people to attend – and that's easier said than done. The solution is to ensure that the event is of genuine interest and value to the prospective audience. Make sure you have something meaningful to say. Use a relevant, well-known guest speaker to add attractiveness if necessary.

Limited coverage

Seminars offer a great sales opportunity, but only with a limited number of prospects. Audiences are often counted in tens rather than hundreds or thousands. Thus, seminars are useful where we are targeting small numbers of people but of little value in mass markets. The cost and logistics of running enough seminars to create effective coverage of a volume market are unsustainable.

DEMONSTRATING THE BENEFITS

We cannot consider this aspect of communication without paying testimony to one of the most valuable features of exhibitions and seminars. We can allow people to see, touch, and if relevant, smell and taste our products.

Consumer marketers can trial everything from new food products to the latest electric drill range. Capital goods manufacturers can demonstrate heavy equipment which cannot be easily transported to customers' premises. Car manufacturers and many others can test reaction to new product concepts.

For many brands, this 'real-life' experience by prospective customers is an important element of effective communication.

PUBLICISING OUR PARTICIPATION

Rather as with sponsorship activity, the costs here don't end with the actual event. Or at least, if they do, we fail to capitalise on the potential available.

We must have a strategy in place to attract prospects to our stand, to come and hear our conference paper or to visit our seminar. Again, we see links to our other communication activities; we may use direct mail, advertising or other techniques to do this job. We should certainly ensure our PR activity is supporting our participation.

The work continues at the event itself. We must work the crowd to good effect. Face-to-face communication will be critical if we are to get the most out of our investment.

After the event, the costs continue to mount. Good follow-up procedures are essential to convert contacts into customers. Abstracts of papers should be widely circulated. News releases and interviews should be organised. We might consider preparing a video of the seminar for loan to those who did not attend. If we had something of real interest to say, we could prepare a video news release for TV use.

11

Electronic Communication

Electronic media are opening up a whole, challenging new world to marketing. The Internet, with developments such as Intranets and Extranets, is creating new channels, not only for communication but also for every aspect of marketing.

Readers should be familiar with the Internet – a global public channel which is already providing information that is mind-boggling in its range and depth of information. An Intranet is simply a closed user group version of the same thing. Typically, a major company with a number of locations would use an Intranet for many of its communication needs amongst colleagues. An Extranet is a kind of half-way house; typically, a business might set up an Extranet accessible only to a select group such as customers or distributors.

INTERNAL MARKETING

Any electronic medium is only as good as its underlying information. After all, the medium is no more than that: a delivery mechanism. However, if we have the right information in place, an intranet can be a superb tool for internal communication and marketing.

FAQ (frequently asked questions) sites can be of significant help to the salesforce. The marketing communication part of the site can keep all staff up to date with plans, events and news, while the intranet can play a major role in cascading information throughout the business. International offices can download, for example, original advertising source material electronically – clearly beneficial in terms of cost and speed. And, of course, the ubiquitous e-mail helps general communication.

These are just a few examples of the multitude of benefits which can be had from a well constructed intranet.

EASIER TO DO BUSINESS WITH

An extranet can make a real difference to how efficiently we do business with customers. This takes us into the realm of e-commerce, as it has become known.

At a simple level, we could allow customers to access company and product information whenever and wherever they wish. Furthermore, we could allow them access to internal systems which would let them check delivery status, their account position and other information. At its most sophisticated, we might have links to, for example, a retailer's EFTPOS system. As a business partner, we receive real time information on how our products are selling through their outlets. As their stock levels diminish, the computer automatically triggers an order for replacement stock, advises the manufacturing control system, sees the process through to delivery and issues an electronic invoice – which is, naturally, paid by electronic bank transfer.

This is no longer pie-in-the-sky. One company that I advise has sensors in several customers' storage tanks. The IT system is constantly calculating average usage of raw material and, when levels reach a pre-set number of days' stock, a top-up delivery is triggered.

Extranets are changing how we interact with customers commercially. In major accounts, suppliers who fail to keep up with these developments will find that there are customers where they can no longer trade. Expertise in e-commerce will be an entry point for doing business.

EVERYBODY'S INTERNET

The Internet itself is truly a phenomenon. Use is growing exponentially; it cuts across geographies, cultures and social classes; it is global, almost universally accessible at low cost, and more or less completely unregulated.

The Net, as it is often called, is a challenge and opportunity to all its users. It has already become a fairly significant advertising medium, both in the sense that it carries paid advertisements and in that it provides a platform for brand publicity within our own sites, and the most popular sites are attracting tens of thousands of visitors each day. However, site design is something approaching a black art! The medium is in its infancy but has already gone through three or four generations of design concept, and the harsh reality is that the majority of sites on the Net are not worth a second visit. Companies rushed to establish a presence – with no rules, experience or standards to guide them. Very many have become disillusioned and have withdrawn, but, as a bank of experience is becoming established, and specialists are building and selling their knowledge, such companies will come back with fuller and better offerings.

There is no doubt that the best sites (and the 'best' changes almost daily – check specialist magazines for those worth looking at, or check the Net!) do enhance the brand and deliver its values. They also deliver customer value and that's the key to generating repeat visits.

THE DECISION TO GO UP

The Internet brings a unique level of one-to-one interactivity to our communication. We can converse with individual customers or prospects in real time, something only face-to-face selling can achieve otherwise; it can carry a brand message in an involving and different manner to any other medium; it can liven the brand in the same way as is achieved by television and radio. If aspects such as these form part of the communication objectives, then the Net is worthy of consideration. If not, then forget it. As with any other technique, it should only be used if it fits the plan – not just because it's a good idea or everyone else is doing it.

Establishing a presence need not cost a fortune. A very basic site can be established for virtually nothing, using capacity bundled with an Internet subscription and designed within a word processing package. At the next level, a simple commercial site can cost as little as a few thousand pounds. However, a significant site, with multiple links and attractive interactive elements can demand an investment well into six figures. And the costs are not one-off: maintaining and developing a big site to keep it attractive and competitive can require a budget running into six figures a year. Obviously, we need to look carefully at the payback in terms of added brand value before leaping into such expenditure.

THE MARKETING CHALLENGE

These new media pose challenges way beyond the confines of the communication aspects of marketing. Already the world's biggest bookshop is to be found on the Net. Dell computers take several million dollars per day in revenue from their site. Similarly, a great deal of software is sold via the Net, for instant download.

The Internet will change the face of marketing in the coming years. Car dealers in the USA are finding consumers surfing the Net to get the best price on a model they have already selected in the showroom. The Euro, combined with the harmonisation of rates of Value Added Tax, will give complete pricing transparency across Europe. This will cause major changes in business: global branded products will be ordered from the most competitive source. Easy comparison and on-line ordering are likely to force us to find new ways of differentiating a retail offering. Businesses will be able to compare potential suppliers without having to take a currency risk into comparison, and will use the Net as a vehicle to help make the comparisons. Software is already available which enables key word searching and price ranking and e-commerce will demand a re-think into how we carry out almost every aspect of doing business.

GETTING IT RIGHT

Even in such a fast developing media area, there are already some useful ground rules:

- Start by getting the objectives and the purpose clearly focused – and by measuring the likely value to accrue from the effort.
- Find out what the customer would consider valuable.
- Design the information before you design the site – make sure you will deliver value which will be seen as such by your market.
- Ensure that the site will work efficiently for the visitor, within the constraints of contemporary technology.
- Invest enough to create a site that counts in comparison to key competitors.
- Keep it fresh with regular updates and changes.
- Finally, review the strategic marketing implications of the whole media area for your business.

AND THERE'S MORE

It's not only the Internet and related technology that is changing the face of marketing communication. Developments in digital television will eventually lead to the consumer having the ability to tailor an evening's viewing to his or her own wishes. It will also, however, enable advertisers to tailor their approach. The same programme might be broadcast in many countries but carry different advertising in each.

The continuing fragmentation of media is making it more difficult to reach some audiences but, when we can track them down, it allows us to make a more individual approach to smaller, more targeted audience segments.

12

Arming the Salesforce

In our excitement at dealing with the 'glamorous' elements of communication – such as the next TV or press campaign – we often pay only scant regard to the communication needs of our sales people. Yet, in any business, they are central to our ability to get results. That fact is self-evident in markets such as capital goods or major turnkey projects. These are sales which typically take months to close and, in exceptional cases, can take literally years. The importance of the sales person's role is crystal clear.

However, even at the other extreme, low value fast moving consumer goods, we forget the sales team at our peril.

Only a small proportion of goods go from factory to the end-user without sales effort of some kind. Taking the broad view of an economy, the vast majority of products go through a distribution chain of some kind. Thus, sales professionals are needed to help them on their way.

Marketing communication can make the job easier. Even a multiple retailer such as Tesco or Safeway will take the possible stocking of a brand seriously if the brand owner proposed to put £20 million behind advertising it. Sadly, most of us are not in the position of having such a persuasive argument to lean on and so our sales teams have to work somewhat harder.

WHO IS RESPONSIBLE?

Arming the salesforce is a significant, and can be a major, task.

Elements of their needs may be met from several sources within the company. The training department will be involved in honing the professional selling skills. Part of that may involve assembling the sales arguments. Sales management will definitely have a role in determining the best way to close the sale.

I firmly believe that the marketing communications team should be heavily involved at a number of points. It is they who are the guardians of the brand image, the brand identity and the consistency of the messages being delivered. How can they fulfil that role without input into what the salesforce is saying out there in the market?

To identify where that involvement should occur, let's examine some of the various stages in a customer relationship. Figure 12.1 shows the stages.

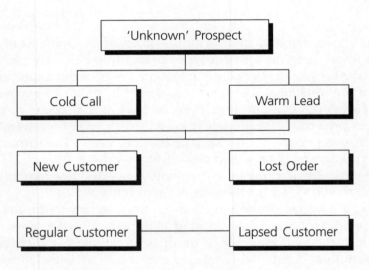

Figure 12.1 *The stages of a customer relationship*

The 'unknown' prospect, in the context of this model, is the one we have not met face to face. Our task at this point is to 'warm' the prospect; to predispose them positively towards the brand. For that we use the full panoply of techniques covered in these chapters.

The sales person then achieves that all-important first meeting. It could be a 'cold' call, that is, initiated by the sales person, or a 'warm' lead, perhaps as a result of the prospect responding to an advertisement or piece of direct mail. In either case, we can ensure that our information library is equipped to allow the sales person to find out a great deal about the prospect prior to the meeting. We might provide directories or on-line databases to meet this need.

That information will enable the sales person to prepare his or her presentation to suit the perceived needs of the prospect.

Where we approach a warm lead, we should provide details of how the lead arose, which product advertisement attracted the prospect's attention and prompted the enquiry.

In both cases, the sales person will need adequate product and company information, possibly in several forms. We must understand the dynamics of the selling situation and provide anything which will help improve the chances of putting the order in the bag.

When we win a new customer, we should seek to reinforce the win through small – though by no means insignificant – gestures, such as an appropriately worded 'thank you' letter. You, the communication expert, must provide such items.

If the initial order is lost, you need a mechanism for keeping that prospect informed and thinking positively about the brand. They will come back into the market at some point and this interim work will make eventual conversion to sale much more likely. The same is true of lapsed customers.

The salesforce is unlikely to have the time to keep in regular contact with all companies or people in this category. It's a communication job which the marketing communications team should undertake.

The sales role with existing customers falls into two parts: account management – nurturing the relationship – and business development. Marketing communication can be in touch with customers when the sales person cannot. We can mail or phone them more often, more cheaply, than the sales person can visit. In business development, we can provide case study materials on what we have done for company A to help break into its sister companies.

So, at every stage, there is a valuable communication job to be done, which is often outside the time availability or scope of the person actually selling.

A LOOK IN THE TOOLBOX

Figure 12.2 paints a pen portrait of a notional company. It has two divisions, one of which sells direct to its ends users, while the second sells through wholesalers and retailers to its consumers. This is a common shape in industrial companies. In consumer goods companies, we could view the divisions as being major account sales and distributor sales respectively. To deliver against the needs of

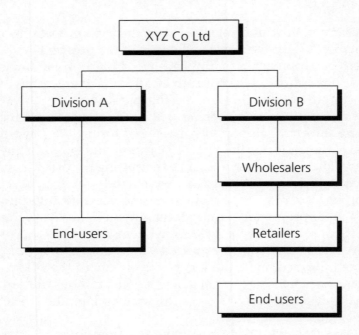

Figure 12.2 *The XYZ company*

both sales forces requires an extensive toolkit. The outline given below shows just how much communications can offer to help make those vital sales.

EXTERNAL INFORMATION

We can provide information on prospects, as stated earlier, in the form of company directories or on-line databases. We can keep the salesforce up to date with events in the client company through press clipping services or on-line business news services. It makes a good first impression on a prospect and it generates respect from clients when sales people can show their homework and a real interest in the client.

Market reports can either be bought off the shelf or specially commissioned. Such information can be invaluable in targeting the salesforce at the right prospects (and for many other marketing purposes).

Information on competitors and their current activity let the team know what they are up against. Knowing your enemy, as any good general will tell you, is one of the keys to winning a war. Keep files of competitive advertising and news on competitors. It's gold dust.

COMPANY, BRAND AND PRODUCT INFORMATION

Any sales person must be able to talk knowledgeably about their own company. They need to understand the mission statement and the broad strategy which the business or the brand is pursuing. Typically, this is contained in the Annual Report and the corporate brochure.

They must know 'who's who in the zoo'. Keep the organisation chart current. There's nothing worse than having a member of the sales team not know where to guide a customer for help, or where to find an answer to a problem quickly and efficiently.

Sales literature must be benefit led. Customers don't buy the features of a product. They buy what it will do for them. When heavy technical information has to be delivered, confine it to appropriate data sheets. Don't let it clog up the benefit message.

A consistent sales message

Successful sales come from a good product, well presented. Make sure the selling 'platform' is carefully constructed to emphasise the benefits of the brand. Then, together with colleagues in Training, ensure everyone is telling the same, consistent, effective story.

That story must be the same as we are delivering through all other elements of our communication activity.

Keep sending the good news

One big problem in maintaining customer relationships is finding legitimate reasons to contact those customers frequently without being a nuisance. Marketing communication can provide fresh and interesting information which overcomes that problem.

Newsletters are one possible solution. When the market is of reasonable size, regular printing of a newsletter becomes a viable, indeed a low cost means of keeping in regular contact.

Monthly updates of advertising and PR activity are very useful to the salesforce. And of course it is compulsory that you send them copies of every new advertisement – before it appears and a customer shows it to them. Copies of PR published about the brand fall into the same category.

In a more structured vein, a regular flow of successful case studies builds a real armoury for the good sales person. Nothing tips the scales more effectively than material which proves that you can indeed deliver what you claim.

Professional presentation

With current IT technology, there is simply no excuse for poor presentation materials, even for small companies. For a few hundred pounds, we can equip a PC with Microsoft Powerpoint or a similar piece of software which will produce first-class results.

Nowadays the options in presentation style are legion. We can use simple overhead or 35mm slides. Presenting by computer allows us more flexibility. We can prepare the 'overhead slides' but leave them in the magic box. Then we can add colour and transition effects to bring them to life. Add colour photographs, scanned in to the PC, and everything takes on a real-life quality. We can even go all the way to a full multimedia presentation using sound, video, still pictures and text without breaking the bank.

We can and should put the sales person in a position to deliver a polished and professional presentation to every customer and prospect.

VALUE ON TAP

The advent of the Internet has created phenomenal opportunities that add value for the customer during the selling process.

Powerful database tools, such as Lotus Notes, allow businesses to marshal their internal knowledge in a much more meaningful and useable way than ever before. Delivery mechanisms such as Intranet, Extranet and Internet (see Chapter 11) let us put that information at the sales professional's disposal – even during a customer visit. A laptop and a cellular phone, for example, let the sales person dial into company systems and retrieve information in 'real time' in front of the customer or prospect. Everything from product information to delivery and account status is at their fingertips. Service personnel can use the same technology to solve problems on the spot – problems which otherwise would take much longer to deal with.

Thanks to the march of technology, marketing communicators are well advised to live closely with their IT colleagues. The enabling power of IT in the field of marcoms is advancing at a frightening rate.

GIVE THE SALESFORCE THE ATTENTION THEY'RE DUE

It is a serious mistake to leave the salesforce as an afterthought in our communication planning. What they say, what they show and what they leave behind with the customer must be fully integrated with everything else we do. They are our front line with the customer. If they sing from a different hymn book than the rest of us, they could damage the whole selling process.

13

Sales Promotion

A definition:

> Sales promotion comprises a range of tactical marketing techniques designed within a strategic marketing framework to add value to a product or service in order to achieve specific sales and marketing objectives.

That's a mouthful to begin with! It comes from the Institute of Sales Promotion but, while I hesitate to comment on the views of that august body, it's a definition which tells us little. It may even be misleading in describing sales promotion as tactical; there are companies such as Allied Carpets whose whole strategy is based on promotion activity.

Sales promotion is a technique which has significant potential to improve short-term sales and, like direct response work, its effectiveness can be tightly measured. Although its strategic value is the subject of considerable debate, nevertheless it is an important tool of marketing. There are few markets or products where it cannot be used and few brands to which it cannot be applied.

It might be argued that the subject should be confined to books on marketing rather than on marketing communication. However, the use of sales promotion can have a profound effect on the perception of the brand and therefore should be included here.

To those who doubt the potential impact on brand values, I recommend reading the contemporary material on the Hoover 'free flights' fiasco at the start of the 1990s. That particular sales promotion scheme generated enough negative publicity to keep a large crisis handling team occupied for a long time. It cost the company an estimated £20 million to put right and certainly damaged the brand.

Almost every company and brand uses sales promotion at some point. That use can vary from special offers to the consumer to incentive schemes through the distribution chain.

In this chapter we'll look briefly at the main types of promotion as identified in Figure 13.1, then consider the benefits offered by the technique.

Irrespective of the market area, promotions can generally be categorised as one of five main types:

1. price promotions;
2. those offering extra product (in the business market, this might be additional services related to the basic product);
3. premium offers;
4. charity schemes; and
5. those promotions offering the opportunity to win prizes.

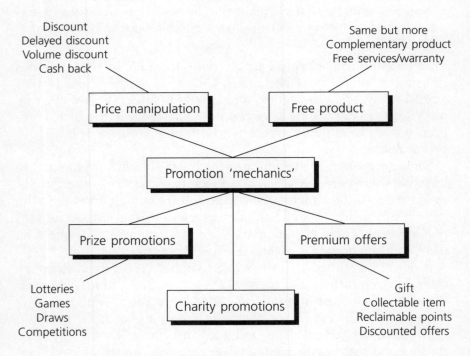

Figure 13.1 *The main types of sales promotion*

MANIPULATING PRICE

Walk down any shopping street and you will be confronted with ranks of 'sale' signs. In these post-recessionary times we seem to have acquired the skill of running the January sales straight into the spring and Easter sales which then continue seamlessly through the summer and autumn sales all the way to the big Christmas 'special'.

These straightforward discounted offers are the most common manifestation of the price offer but there are many others.

On the supermarket shelf we find not only the '5p off this pack' offer but also offers of money off the next purchase, the latter aimed at stimulating repeat purchase. Another variant is the discount coupon, distributed in various ways including door-to-door drops, at the checkout and in magazines.

The measurability of these offers varies with the specific method used. A discounted price is the most simple to measure in terms of net cost per unit and break-even point for the promotion. We know the margin reduction caused by the discount. We can calculate the cost of publicising the promotion. Therefore we can easily work out the volume increase which we must achieve to gain a return on the effort.

This becomes more difficult with the other forms since each depends on the percentage of those eligible who actually take up the offer. Even if we are prompted to purchase by a special offer which promises something at a later stage, many of us – through simple inertia – will not get around to using our entitlement. This can make the delayed offer more financially attractive to run. The corollary is that delayed offers are generally not so effective as those which give immediate reward.

The final form worthy of specific mention in this section is the 'cash back' offer. This can be seen as a delayed discount deal. The form is growing, particularly in the financial and computer sectors but has been seen in recent years in many other categories.

Each of these promotions can be found in business markets. Volume discounts, late delivery penalties, retrospective cumulative volume deals, and marketing funding based on the level of business are all price promotions of one shape or another.

SAME PRICE, MORE PRODUCT

The bottle of shampoo declaring '25 per cent extra – FREE', the special offer on beer giving '8 for the price of 6' – both are prime examples of the something-for-nothing promotion involving extra product. The approach is by no means confined to downmarket brands either. As I write, local stores have such offers on premium lagers and cases of wine; and the clothing store Hornes will give you a second suit free with each suit you buy.

Another approach encourages cross-selling of a related product from the same stable. The cosmetics market is fertile ground for such offers: buy the perfume and receive the face cream free. This can be extended into alliances between different manufacturers where complementary products are involved. For example, a manufacturer of pasta might offer a free trial jar of another manufacturer's Bolognese sauce.

THE FREE GIFT

Some readers may be old enough to remember the 'classic' premium of the 1960s: the free plastic daffodil. For those too young to remember, be grateful. Fortunately the premium market has matured since then. Even the millions of wine glasses given by the petrol companies in the 1980s were genuinely usable.

Such programmes are now highly sophisticated – and clearly aimed at building repeat and regular business. We now have schemes such as Air Miles which has gone beyond its original concept and now allows value to be built through a wide range of purchases, the 'winnings' eventually being taken as free airline tickets.

Not all premium products are free; many are offered at a substantial discount on the normal retail price. The typical form is, for example, collect six tops from soft drinks cans and send them with money for a music compact disc, the price being perhaps half or less of the perceived value of the premium product.

THE 'FEEL GOOD' FACTOR

The ethical consumer is becoming more of a reality in the 1990s. This has given rise to an increasing number of sales promotions linked to charitable contributions. This normally involves the seller or manufacturer donating a certain amount of money to a nominated charity for each product sold. Such offers can be tied in neatly with charitable sponsorship activities undertaken by the manufacturer. Like the straight discount, they are expensive in the sense that there is an extra cost on every single product sold. So far, experience suggests that this type of promotion is not as effective as a price discount. However, that is a generalisation and the approach may be extremely effective for target audiences whose members exhibit a particularly high degree of social awareness and conscience.

Charity-linked promotions can also contribute to building particular brand characteristics in conjunction with other communication efforts.

THE HOLIDAY OF A LIFETIME . . .

Or it could be a new house, a new car or something less spectacular. The prize promotion has been around a long time.

They are attractive to the organiser in that – in terms of prize cost – they are predictable and containable yet capable of generating high levels of interest. But beware! There are some interesting legal complexities in this area. Indeed there are actually four types of promotion defined by law under this broad heading: lotteries, competitions, games and draws.

Before launching such a venture, take advice from the Institute of Sales Promotion or a reputable, specialist sales promotion agency.

APPLYING PROMOTIONS

As may be evident from the above, sales promotion can help achieve a number of types of objective:

- It can encourage new product trial.
- It can raise the level of repeat purchases.
- It can help build customer loyalty by establishing a pattern of regular purchasing of the brand.
- It can motivate distributors and their sales forces.

However, it is not the cure for all ills.

Gains made during a sales promotion are tough to hold on to. It may be because promotions tend to attract 'promiscuous' consumers who are likely to switch brands again at the first smell of a better offer. Hence the debate about the validity of the technique as a strategic rather than a tactical weapon.

Globalising promotions can be extremely difficult or impossible depending on the particular type of promotion envisaged. Figure 13.2 gives a glimpse of just some of the national differences in what is allowed by law in particular countries. And that's without considering the cultural differences which may make one promotion effective in, say, the UK but completely ineffective in another country.

Promotion	UK	Ger	Bel	Lux	Aus	Nor	Swi
Price discount	✓	✓	✓	✓	✓	✓	✓
Discount voucher	✓	✗	✓	?	?	✗	✗
Cash back	✓	?	✓	✗	?	?	✗
Extra product	✓	?	?	✓	?	?	?
Free product	✓	✓	?	✓	✓	✓	✓
In-pack premium	✓	?	✓	✗	?	✗	✗
Collectables	✓	?	?	✗	✗	✗	✗
Discounted product	✓	✓	✓	✗	✓	✓	✗
Competition	✓	?	✓	?	?	?	✓
Free draw	✓	✗	✗	✗	✗	✗	✗

Figure 13.2 *Some of the variations in law across Europe*

Despite its shortcomings, sales promotion does have a valid and valuable role to play. In addition to the applications mentioned earlier, it can bring a certain indefinable and certainly unmeasurable element to the mix: it can create excitement and 'street noise' around the brand. But this will occur only if the audience is aware of the promotion – which brings us to another key aspect.

DO YOUR MATHEMATICS

I don't propose to go into the whole subject of costing promotions in this book but I will mention the communication aspects of cost.

In-store promotions can be successful with no more than some point-of-sale material to support them. It may be enough to accept existing store traffic and seek to win market share through the on-shelf appeal of the special offer.

Other promotions demand much more, and may themselves result in a full communication plan and major expenditure. In such a case, the promotion can be treated as the 'product' and the plan developed on that basis. That's why we should recognise that, in essence, this is a marketing rather than communication technique. Yet it communicates a great deal about the brand and the effect of the type of promotion used must be the result of careful consideration of that effect. It is for this reason that the communication expert within the company should have a voice at the sales promotion planning table.

14

Selecting the Right Techniques

The preceding chapters are far from being an exhaustive look at each of the options facing us. Each of these techniques of communication demands considerable further study in its own right; a recommended reading list is given at the end of the book. However, the information given in this volume is enough to provide a broad view of the characteristics of each option and leads us to looking at how to select the lead technique and build in others to provide a complete campaign.

The start point is to assess each option against our specific needs and objectives. Figure 14.1 rates each approach against a number of criteria. *Do not take this chart as Gospel truth.* The scoring given (from 1 to 5, where 5 is excellent) would vary depending on the audience, the market and your position in the market. The chart serves only as an indicator of the major strengths of each technique.

ADVERTISING

Advertising can be an extremely cost-effective method of communicating with mass audiences. The range of media available means we can normally find the right combination for any mass audience at an acceptable cost per thousand (CPT) people reached.

However, we should differentiate between broadcast and specialist media. The former, including national press, TV and radio, offer extensive coverage. The latter is usually made up of smaller-

	Large audience	Small audience	Regional/Global	Local/National	Short-term sales	Brand building	Impact/prestige
Advertising: broadcast	5	2	4	5	4	5	5
Advertising: specialist	2	4	4	5	3	4	4
PR/media relations	5	5	5	5	3	3	4
Direct marketing	3	4	2	4	5	2	3
Relationship marketing	4	5	4	5	3	5	3
Sponsorship	5	3	5	5	1	5	5
Design	5	5	5	5	1	4	3
Arming the salesforce	3	5	5	5	4	3	2
Sales promotion	5	5	2	5	5	3	3

Figure 14.1 *Assessing lead technique candidates*

circulation magazines which cover specialist audiences fairly well – but building mass audience coverage by using large numbers of them may not be cost-effective.

Advertising can offer regional and global coverage using combinations of indigenous and, for example, pan-European press. The growth in electronic media TV is improving this position further.

Retail advertisers such as W H Smith will argue strongly that advertising can have a short-term effect on sales. Indeed in this sector, if the tills don't start ringing the day the advertisement appears, something is wrong with the campaign. Of course, this itself is too much of a blanket statement. It is the case when WHS are advertising their 'back to school' products at the right season, but if they were to launch a campaign aimed more at building the brand than selling specific products, the immediate effect would be much less noticeable.

This brings us to one of advertising's greatest strengths, building enduring brand values. When we think of some of the real long-stay brands such as Dulux, PG Tips, Tetley, Milk Tray and so on, we bring to mind immediately the dog, the chimps, the T-men and the man in black. Advertising – using a great creative idea – has been a major factor in the longevity of these brands.

And prominent advertising *does* add value and prestige to the product, brand and company. It makes the purchase acceptable by moving the brand out of the 'unheard of' category. The judgement of friends and peers on our purchases is important to all of us in some degree or other. A well-exposed brand, particularly one which has been seen on TV, has automatic credibility. This same feature is seen in business markets. That is the basic reason why branded computers still greatly outsell 'clones', even at higher prices. When we buy a brand, we invest our trust, and we rarely trust something we do not know.

PR AND MEDIA RELATIONS

Effective media work can help us reach any audience – except hermits! We all read, watch or listen to some communication medium pretty much every day. This applies everywhere except perhaps in particularly poor cultures which are unlikely, in any event, to be the focus of our business attention.

This form of publicity is not naturally regarded as a booster of short-term sales but it certainly can achieve that. The right product test result in an influential computer magazine, or a 'best buy' rating in a publication like *Which* magazine, can have a dramatic and rapid effect on sales volume.

Regular and positive coverage in appropriate media can aid brand building significantly. And the credibility of the third-party nature of PR can add prestige to the brand, although lacking the impact which advertising can create.

Intelligent use of press relations can deliver impressive results even on modest budgets. Where money is particularly tight, it can be the only viable option. We trade off message control for more extensive coverage than we might be able to afford using other techniques.

DIRECT MARKETING

Direct marketing can cover all audiences well, depending on the technique used to deliver it. The comments relating to advertising apply when that is used. The other main method of delivery is direct mail.

Such is the quality of consumer lists available for hire in most markets that we can now segment an audience by age, sex, geography, lifestyle, attitudes, purchasing history and other qualifying factors. So we can use it for most types of audience. (It is worth noting that business lists are rarely as detailed or kept as well up to date as the best consumer lists.)

However, the bigger the audience and the wider the international spread, the more difficult it becomes to carry out cost-effective direct mail. Yet it can and does work for certain brands on such a scale.

Some direct mail is kept and responded to at a later date, but the vast majority of response comes quickly. It can improve sales in very short order indeed – after the mailing has gone out. We do need to take into account the development and production time in assessing this point. When time is of the essence, a black and white advertisement for national press can be turned around and in the newspaper within a day or two. In contrast, a serious direct mail campaign can be weeks in the preparation.

RELATIONSHIP MARKETING

When we get it right, relationship marketing can score well across all of the criteria listed. The problem is in getting it right.

Many so-called relationship programmes are little more than thinly disguised sales promotions. The best, such as some of the airline 'executive clubs', are built on a sound strategy which offers real added value to the customer, and over a long period. These may genuinely be referred to as loyalty schemes because that is what they achieve.

Relationship marketing is often a major plank in communication strategy but is rarely the lead activity. Its obvious shortcoming is that it concentrates almost exclusively on retention of existing customers rather than on prospecting for new ones.

Having said that, American Express has consistently won a proportion of new card holders through a member-get-member scheme which might fairly be described as part of a relationship marketing programme. In this system, card holders who recruit a friend to Amex receive a gift in return. Interestingly, although this was where the company started its relationship marketing, it has developed this area with the introduction of a long-term points scheme where *every* use of the card is rewarded.

SPONSORSHIP

The scores allocated are largely self-explanatory. But they are generally true for brands which are already well known. Sponsorship is acting as a support to a communication strategy which has already built a certain level of awareness and which is delivering the right messages in other ways. The sponsorship is providing more opportunities for the market to meet the brand.

Sponsorship effort on poorly recognised brands is largely wasted; simple recognition of the company name is unlikely to make a significant difference to our market position.

That does not mean that sponsorship is only for big companies. If your target audience is local, and you are known in that particular market, providing free football strips to the local boy scout team could be a worthwhile investment.

In essence, sponsorship might be a viable candidate to lead a campaign for established brands but is likely only to work as a support activity otherwise.

DESIGN

Good design would rarely be regarded as a lead technique. In those companies really committed to it, it is simply 'something that we do'; it runs through how their offices look and the design of their products to the look of their literature, packaging and advertising. It is a driving force of their approach to life, an attitude which underpins how they approach many projects, including communication.

However, there are cases where design as a communication tool has made all the difference in the marketplace. A powerful example can be found in the packaging arena. The market share in sales of ladies' tights won by Boots against Marks & Spencer in the early 1990s can be clearly shown to result from a redesign of their packaging.

In sectors where little real product differentiation exists, the communication itself can become the differentiator. The campaigns for Benson & Hedges and Silk Cut cigarettes are two of the relatively few examples where design could be argued to be the core of the communication.

ARMING THE SALESFORCE

This should be the first thing any of us does. If we are not well prepared to sell effectively, we should not begin to contemplate an external communication programme. Enough said!

SALES PROMOTION

The technique offers enough different 'mechanics' to find one suitable for any audience. The promotion can be communicated through all of the other techniques listed.

However, the law varies from country to country in respect of what types of promotion are permissible. This limits our ability to run, for example, a truly pan-European campaign.

The value of promotions in building brands is the subject of some debate. There are those who argue that the 'gimmicky' nature of promotions devalues the brand. The counter view is that a well-chosen promotion can actually reinforce brand values. I tend to support the latter view. I believe that sales promotion in itself cannot build enduring brands but, when used in concert with other techniques and kept strictly in line with brand strategy, it can support the development of the target brand values.

At the same time, promotions can offer high impact if effectively publicised – and, for the reasons given above, may enhance the brand's prestige.

It is difficult to list sales promotion as a lead communication technique, however, since it requires other methods to make the effort visible to the market. As stated in Chapter 13, it is more of a marketing tool than a specific communication tool.

SO HOW DO WE CHOOSE?

The first point we must appreciate is that there is no 'right' answer. For any given market situation there will be numerous ways of using the different communication techniques in an effective mix. Judgement is everything; if you don't have the knowledge and the experience – and the proposed budget is significant for your business – buy the judgement of relevant experts. If the budget is not significant, you may choose to risk trial and error.

The solution is found by going back to the objectives and matching the characteristics of the method to what we expect communication to achieve. Let's look at two very different, imaginary situations and at the possible outcomes of this approach.

The new product launch

We have on our hands a revolutionary new software package which could have a major impact on the whole personal computer market. It is aimed at the business and small office/home office (SoHo) markets. The communication strategy might go through these stages:

1. We need to get the product out into a real-world test (known as beta testing). The ideal technique is face-to-face meetings with a few loyal customers to demonstrate the product and show the result of our market research. The objective is to sign a number of them up as test sites.
2. We want to fire up the salesforce in advance. So we prepare the selling tools and launch both the product and the tools at a special sales conference.
3. We need to prepare our distribution and get them worked up about selling the new product. We could use direct mail, either in a special mailer or through an existing newsletter for dealers and distributors.
4. Ideally, we want the market screaming for the product as soon as it becomes available. We know we are well ahead of the competition in this field of development, so there is little risk in priming a few influential journalists in advance. The coverage generated will create demand in advance of the public launch.

    We expect media coverage to be sustainable for up to three months after launch date because the revolutionary nature of the product will generate a high level of interest.

    For this first quarter, media relations will be our lead activity.
5. The distributors need to see the product being supported.

    It is a wide target audience which is difficult to reach cost-effectively through specialist media. We also want to take the high ground in the market so we need prestigious publicity. Therefore we'll use national press advertising, initially fairly sparingly to complement the media coverage (and show the distributors we're supporting it), but building up to a heavy-weight ad campaign in the following nine months.
6. We need to keep the momentum going, but the product will be

well established by the year end and distributors and dealers will themselves advertise it. The solution could be to develop a cooperative advertising policy where we pay a contribution towards their advertising – provided they feature our brand prominently and in an agreed manner.

7. There will be many customers new to our brand; they are prospective buyers of our other products. So we introduce an incentive to register the software with us, combined with a relationship marketing package which offers ongoing help and information and acts as a promotion vehicle for the rest of the product range.

Attacking a major brand

We are confident that our new soft drink can win market share among 16–24 year olds. But it's a tough market to break into, characterised by big players with high advertising spends. We can't take them on head to head so we have identified a niche positioning as a fashionable drink to certain types of people. Our research shows this is acceptable.

Product availability will be low initially so we'll test market in the Midlands, to meet projected demands.

This is a difficult challenge because the brand needs street credibility – something which is hard to create.

1. We might lead with regional TV advertising to give peer group acceptance and rapid but localised coverage in the test market area. We would buy spots which occurred in programmes very specific to the character of the target audience.
2. We might support this with sponsorship of events in the three or four trendiest nightspots in the region and publicise these using local radio – again around appropriate programmes.
3. Sales promotion could boost the effort by developing an associated offer of a T-shirt specially designed to appeal to the target group.

In each of these cases, our choice of communication method is led by three things: our detailed understanding of the audience, our knowledge of the marketing objectives and our ability to identify what communication should be doing to help achieve those objectives.

The main options

In every case, arming the salesforce will be important to the success-ful outcome of any sales campaign. Experience of many cases similar to those mentioned above suggests that there are three main options in seeking a lead activity: advertising, press relations and direct mail. Each of these is capable, subject to the particular market circum-stances, of leading a powerful communication strategy.

But the list is not exclusive. For your situation, a series of seminars, or dominance of a few key trade exhibitions or, indeed, straight-forward face-to-face selling to known prospects might be the most effective way of driving your communication effort. A combination of logical thought as described in this chapter, and insight into your own market and audience should take you to a workable choice of lead technique.

ADDING THE ELEMENTS

Both of the notional cases given show how a number of techniques can be assembled to ensure that the complete job is done.

Having identified how we will lead the campaign, we then assess whether that single approach will achieve everything we need to do. It rarely will. Typically, a 'one-legged' approach will miss part of the audience, or a stage of the marketing process, or part of the geographic coverage we seek, or be unsuited to conveying all of the message.

We must then look to other techniques to fill the communication gap, gradually building the total picture for our audience.

Having selected the main activity, look for the holes in the jigsaw – as seen through the eyes of the target audience. Go back to the matrix given in Chapter 3 (repeated here as Figure 14.2) and build a picture of how your audience will receive particular messages. In this case the headings (A to D or whatever) are the various techniques you will define or add to fill in the blanks. Use your knowledge of the various techniques to support the main activity with others to construct a plan which will deliver the message effectively.

Finally, we have a strategy for each individual campaign.

We now move to the next part of this stage of the process – to produce an outline tactical plan showing the types of advertising

Audience: ....

Message \ Source	A	B	C	D

Figure 14.2 *A plan matrix from the receiver's view*

media we propose to use, the media we will target for PR purposes, the literature we will develop and so on.

As an example, considerations on advertising will require two steps:

1. Consider which medium is best for reaching the particular audience segment under review – TV, newspapers, magazines, trade press, posters and so on.
2. Look at how that particular medium will be used. Which TV programmes should we advertise around? Does the *Sunday Times* offer better coverage than the *Daily Telegraph*?

Next we take a preliminary view on the size or length of advertisement or commercial and on frequency of appearance necessary to do the job. (See Chapter 17 for a view on involving external agencies for advice.)

Then the final element of this part of the process can be drawn up: an overall timing plan which reflects such things as seasonality in our markets, product launch timings, exhibition attendance, press events, outline advertising programme and direct mail plans. Figure 14.3 shows an actual example. From this outline plan, we can develop a first view of the budget necessary to do the job.

Everything is now in place to construct the overview of the integrated campaign.

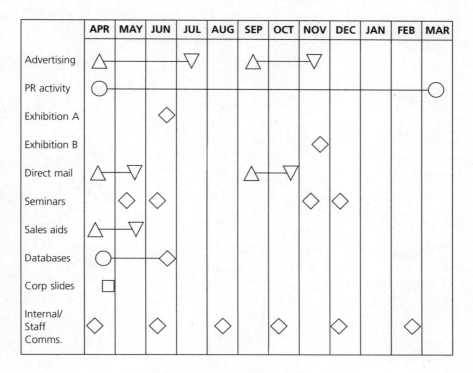

Figure 14.3 *A typical outline tactical plan*

15

Assembling the Total Plan

If you are in a central marketing services department, the next step is to take a look at the proposed total budget. In an ideal world this would go forward for approval by the powers that be. I say 'ideal' because this would result in a completely task-based budget sufficient to support all aspects of the corporate and divisional objectives.

This, however, is a rare circumstance indeed! More likely is that the total is beyond any reasonable budget expectations. And some trimming will be required.

The principle to be applied is 'need to' rather than 'like to'. Review the overall plans and decide whether each of the individual campaigns is absolutely necessary, and if so whether any could be cut back to some extent without too much damage to the overall effort. This will mean going back to the audience list for each campaign and eliminating non-priority audiences and then adjusting the campaign accordingly.

When this has been done, we'll need to look at individual activities within each campaign. Do not, repeat *do not*, make simple across-the-board percentage cuts. You may end up doing all the things you planned but none of them to a sufficient level to have a meaningful effect. It is better to cut some areas of activity to be able to fund the remainder adequately to make a difference.

There is a threshold below which investment in a communication tool becomes pointless. If you cannot afford to run an effective television campaign, reconsider press as an alternative. If you cannot fund a powerful direct mail campaign, don't run a cheap compromise. Do it well or not at all.

The process will cut the total to some extent. If it is still beyond a reasonable figure bearing in mind the commercial position of the company, then the original objectives must be modified. There is little point in cutting further without challenging the objectives. Otherwise, the communication manager is left in the position of promising a level of support and effectiveness which he or she cannot deliver within a viable investment.

CAN WE HANDLE THE WORKLOAD?

Having had budget approval at this stage, we can begin to develop the detail of the total plan.

The needs of each market and division can now be met within the proposal. But can we deliver? We now need to check whether we have the resources to handle the work which we envisage.

In a devolved organisation where each division has its own resources (or perhaps where resources are spread geographically or in subsidiary companies), this might not be a problem. In a centralised department it could be a recipe for disaster.

Compile an overview chart of the major elements of each plan (Figure 15.1) and assess whether you have the staff and/or external agency resources to cope with the load. In the sample shown, the exhibition and seminar programme is particularly heavy. These are time-consuming events from a management viewpoint. Unless there is a large department responsible for the plan, I would be greatly concerned about the ability to handle the programme.

Alternatives to be considered might be re-timing the seminar programme to try to put it into clearer space, or subcontracting the whole exhibition programme (bearing in mind the budget limitations).

A FINAL 'SANITY' CHECK

Now look at Figure 15.2 (reproduced from Figure 3.4).

Early in the process we summarised all of the business's objectives in this form. We have the key audiences and the required geographic coverage on one or two simple sheets. It's time to double-check that the proposal we are about to implement – following all of the stages of revision and internal budget negotiations – will deliver what it must.

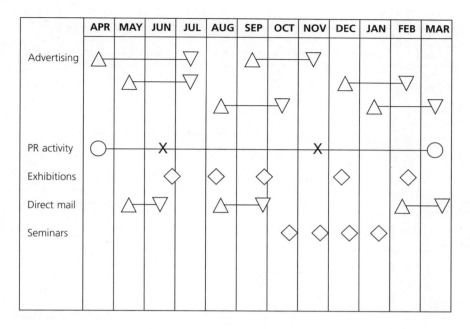

Figure 15.1 *Assessing the resource needs*

Use the form given in Figure 15.2 to view the total activity from an audience perspective. Go through each of the key audiences individually and look at what messages they will be receiving and how those messages will be delivered.

As we planned the individual campaigns, our focus was on the specific needs of that brand or company or division of our business. But we know there is an overlap in audiences, which is why there is a need to integrate our efforts.

We must now be confident that what each audience will receive is the full picture of what we want to deliver and that the messages build a *consistent* picture which will create the desired positioning for the brand. If it does not, go around any necessary parts of the loop once again to iron out any conflicts or fill any gaps. Inevitably, we will be shuffling priorities once more to create budgets to fill those gaps, and we will need to have serious internal discussions about any message conflicts.

The end result should be a plan which, while evidencing some pragmatic compromise, ensures that every penny spent on com-munication adds weight to the total effort and effectiveness and is sharply focused on achieving the company's business objectives.

	Key Audiences	Geography		
Core Campaigns		USA	Europe	Asia
Corporate 1				
Corporate 2				
Functional 1				
Functional 2				
Functional 3				
Business Unit 1				
Business Unit 2				
Business Unit 3				
Product 1				
Product 2				
Product 3				

Figure 15.2 *The final sanity check*

It should be deliverable within available or planned resources. And most importantly, it is designed to deliver a single, consistent positioning and a series of carefully targeted messages which are consistent with that positioning. In short, it is the best communication investment which the company can make within the restrictions of the available funds.

We planned to develop an integrated campaign which met corporate needs and, thus far, we have delivered that campaign.

Now it's time to turn plan into reality.

16

Keeping it all Together

The thought process which has gone into getting this far is absolutely essential to integrated communication. Its outward manifestation is, of course, what appears in public – the campaigns we actually run to reach the target audiences.

Poor quality of thought – or indeed a lack of consideration of the benefits of integration – shows itself in the disparate nature of the various elements of a company's communications.

The symptoms are common. Look at half-a-dozen advertisements for the brand and it looks as if six different companies are doing the advertising. Listen for PR messages which portray a company built on traditional values, clashing with direct mail which positions the brand at the forefront of innovation – with no logical link built between the two messages. Notice how their literature looks and feels different from their advertising or exhibition stand. These differences can be seen not only across elements of the communication mix, but also in differences occurring over time.

In truth, this can also be the case where the thinking *has* been done but the implementation has fallen apart at the seams. That's the final challenge: holding the creative look and the tone of voice true to the brand positioning.

WHY CAMPAIGNS FALL APART

Before identifying how to hold it together, it's important to understand why such inconsistencies creep in to damage the brand. They arise for many reasons, all of them destructive, and they seem to creep in whether we're looking at a single product brand or across a major corporate brand selling into many markets.

A weak knowledge base

Many companies research their markets at a given point in time – rather like an annual MoT test on a car. And like the owner of the older car, once we've got through the 'test', we forget about the certificate and the tester's comments on problems which might occur in the future.

Companies do the same with research. They act on it immediately then put it into a dusty file forever. The result is that their knowledge base is fragmented and they fail to identify trends in opinion which could affect the brand. There's no 'brand bible' which encapsulates the relationship between consumer and brand.

Such a book should exist. It should be part of the induction training for anyone who will work on the brand. It should track the history and current position of the brand's relationships with its market. It is the marker against which all prospective communication work should be measured. If the work does not support that vital relationship, it is wrong. It doesn't matter how brilliant the creative solution is – it is wrong.

But it's not enough for the book to exist. It must be *known* to exist. It must be treated with the reverence it deserves.

No clear guidelines

In some companies, you'll find that the final campaigns lack visual consistency even when the message is constant. There are times when this is appropriate but there are others where it simply confuses the market.

Either way, we need to control the creative policy and that means we need clear guidelines as to what is and is not acceptable. Without them, we cannot complain when an overseas office chooses to run a campaign which sounds and looks completely different from what we feel is right for the personality of the brand.

The people problem

Consumer brand managers seem to move on every five minutes. Business-to-business communication staff tend to stick around a little longer. Yet we are trying to build brands which will endure for decades. We certainly want fresh thinking and new insights in our communication – but what we don't want are 'new brooms'.

We have all seen the new person walk in the door and immediately fire the advertising agency. A new brief is handed out and a new campaign, entirely different to anything which has gone before, is launched. The boss has just appointed the new person and does not want to stifle them from day one. So he or she lets it happen. By the time we realise the campaign is wrong for the brand, the damage is done.

In business communication, a more frequent problem is simple lack of appreciation of the power for good which can be had from communication. It is a low priority activity, delegated to a relatively junior member of staff. They love dealing with agencies. It makes them feel important. So they have lots of agencies and give every piece of literature to a new one. The result is a spaghetti of creative approaches which has no relevance to anything to do with the brand values.

This person is buying pretty pictures, not meaningful communication solutions.

CREATE THE ANCHOR

The anchor is the brand book. A tome which lays down the brand position and the parameters of its relationship with its markets. It makes it clear to everyone what the brand stands for and the direction in which we want to go.

The brand book is law.

Personally, I favour going one step further – particularly for corporate brands – and laying down guidelines for how things will look and feel.

The common stage of this, which most companies do already, is the corporate identity manual. This specifies the key elements such as how the brand name must be presented graphically. Typically it will define logo, stationery design, signage, packaging, vehicle livery and countless other such items.

Where the brand covers a number of products and services, it can and perhaps should be taken further, to the point of giving, for example, a creative framework within which all advertising must be developed. This might simply be a corporate strapline which must appear on all ads. It may be defined typefaces to use for headlines and body text. It might be a border device which appears on all ads. It could even go to the extent of stipulating how language may be employed: are abbreviated forms such as 'we'll' allowable?

Serious publications such as *The Economist* provide their journalists with extensive guidelines in this area precisely because they know how significantly language usage can change the character of a publication.

A set of guidelines eliminates a great deal of debate over what is acceptable. These guidelines need to be well publicised within the company, and consistently enforced.

APPOINT THE GUARDIAN

That enforcement requires someone to take responsibility – to be the guardian of the brand. That individual must be seen to have top management support in controlling quality against the norms set down in the book.

The ultimate authority in this respect should be someone who is likely to be around for a reasonable period. It is difficult to establish consistency if the guardian changes every twelve months. In reality, this guardianship often devolves to the main outside agency, most often the advertising agency. It should not. When it happens, the brand owner is guilty of abdicating control of a major asset, something they would not dream of doing in any other aspect of the business.

DEFINE THE CONTROL MECHANISM

There is little point in implementing a management process which is only triggered after money has been wasted. The guardian therefore needs to consider how, and at which points in the process, to exercise control. Figure 16.1 shows the main stages in the process of developing any communication campaign.

In a smaller company which is developing an integrated approach for the first time, it would probably be right for the communication head to see and approve every brief before work is commissioned. That in itself demands a formal system of written briefs. But that is something which any communication professional should insist on in any event!

Before incurring the time and therefore cost of external specialists, the individual responsible for the particular campaign should complete a briefing form similar to that shown as Figure 16.2. It covers why the campaign is to be run, its quantified objectives, the target

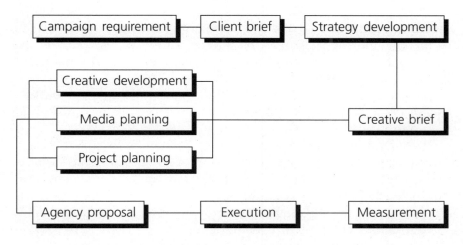

Figure 16.1 *A typical advertising development process*

Project Brief

Project Title: .... Raised by: ....

Project Number: .... Commenced: ....

1. Why do we need this campaign?

2. What must it achieve?

3. Who is the target audience?

4. What is the brand positioning?

5. What is the message of this specific campaign?

6. Why should the audience believe it?

7. How will success be measured?

8. Are there any key target dates?

9. What is the budget allocation?

Signed: .... Approved: ....

Figure 16.2 *Sample internal briefing form*

audience, the brand positioning to be established or supported, the campaign message, the reasons why that message is credible, the measurement of success and the practical elements of timing and budget.

Such a form should be agreed with relevant colleagues, in marketing or product management for example, before being signed off at an appropriate level.

In a small to medium-sized business it may be feasible to check every brief and its progress at each key stage. So the senior person would see the brief, the strategy proposed, and the final proposal for media use and creative solution. (Note that, while I use an advertising example, the stages are similar for any type of communication.)

In a global business of considerable size, perhaps with several communication departments spread around the globe, such a system is likely to prove too cumbersome and will slow down the company's ability to react to market movements. How this is handled depends very much on the level of expertise of the people at the distant sites. If they are highly literate in marketing communication then the best compromise may be to issue the guidelines then review all publicity activity on a regular basis. Inevitably, this will mean some material appearing which falls outside the guidelines. Of course that shouldn't happen – but it always does!

The alternative is to set up a fast response mechanism where each brief is sent by fax or electronic mail to the senior person who undertakes to respond within, say, 24 hours. Likewise, creative or other proposals can be transmitted using IT and turned around with equal alacrity. Such a system keeps a tight rein on standards without holding up the processing of the work by more than a minimum amount.

INTEGRATING THROUGH THE LINE

One tough aspect of holding things together occurs when several external agencies are employed, for example to handle advertising, PR, direct mail and literature design respectively. All agencies tend to suffer from 'NIH': the 'not invented here' syndrome. Good creative talent will always prefer to work without being fettered by the efforts of others. You cannot afford to give them that freedom if you are to get the level of integration you seek.

The optimum solution is to brief the lead technique first. If direct mail is the dominant element of the campaign, ensure that you have the creative solution to that aspect on the table before briefing the other parts. This will make it clear what style and tone of voice is to be achieved by the other specialists. And their work can be held up against the direct mail for comparison and measurement.

The second rule is: keep them talking to each other. Bring the agencies together regularly to review work on the brand in a joint forum. Indeed, where time precludes briefing the main element before the others, then brief all of the work to all those involved at the same time. The discussion of the brief which takes place will benefit everyone – most of all the brand.

MANAGING MULTIPLE PROJECTS

At last we can get on with running real campaigns out there in the marketplace. But the task facing us remains complex. We will be working on a number of fronts at the same time, something which calls for both tight project management and accurate budget control.

The project number is a key tool for keeping things under control. Start every activity with a project reference number which identifies the brand or product involved and the business unit or division for whom the project is being run. Clip the brief to the inside of a project file and use that to hold all estimates, schedules and proposals.

Prepare a project timesheet showing every stage of development, or ideally, prepare a critical path analysis which shows timings and links across all project elements.

If you have the information technology, set up a simple project database and link it to project management software and some personal information management software. All three are available off the shelf and, if you choose a suite from the same manufacturer, should be able to talk to each other with ease.

Such a combination allows you to set up the project, prepare its critical path analysis, then load your diary with reminders on key progress dates.

17

Using External Agencies

Few of us have the luxury of having a full suite of specialist skills in-house. Indeed, it is highly debatable whether we should ever want to. Only the very largest businesses could keep such a range of experts fully occupied, challenged and motivated. Even such big companies are turning back to their core business activities and subcontracting specialist skills as and when they are needed. Fortunately, those skills are readily available for hire.

External input can be applied at several points in the chain of integration. Management consultancies will review the total business and address aspects such as the currently popular 'business process re-engineering'. Beneath this top layer, we find functional specialists who can help with, for example, Total Quality programmes or new product development processes.

Marketing consultancies form one specialist subset.

THE MARKETING COMMUNICATION CONSULTANT

The late 1980s and early 1990s saw a further segmentation and the growth of an even more specialist sector: the marketing communication ('marcom') consultancy. An organisation of this type should be capable of helping a client develop a fully integrated communication strategy from start to finish. Normally, the consultancy will not actually implement the programme (but would have the contacts to introduce you to those who would).

Whether a marcom specialist is used should depend on the in-house skills at your disposal. Against their use is of course the cost involved: as in any field, the best consultants do not come cheaply. In their favour is the fact that they can bring breadth of experience of many markets and businesses which allows them to develop a strategy more quickly, and often with more effectiveness than a relatively inexperienced staff team.

One aspect of that time saving comes from the fact that the consultant is usually working to well-developed models which have been proven with other clients – so the whole process is speeded up by the amount of time it would have taken to design a workable process.

It is also worth bearing in mind that an experienced consultant has been through all the political problems which can crop up when shifting from a free-for-all to a fully integrated programme – and can guide you through that particular minefield.

IMPLEMENTATION ASSISTANCE

Most companies use an advertising or a PR agency at some time. I have grouped such agencies under the general title of implementation assistance. They, too, vary in nature.

At one end of the scale we find the one-stop shop. At the other, major marketing communication groups such as WPP have a network of agencies in each specialist area, which allows them to offer a total service. Much smaller, but still falling into the latter category, is the small provincial agency which also offers to handle everything for its local clients.

Whatever the scale, such shops do make integrated solutions easier to achieve. The solutions for all of the techniques to be used come from one source; they will suffer less from the 'not invented here' problem mentioned in Chapter 16.

The risk is that such agencies can be good generalists but masters of no particular technique. This should not be the case with the global groups; they will normally field several of their specialist agencies in a team assembled for a specific client account. But it can be true of the small local agency.

In the middle of our scale is the specialist agency which concentrates on one or more of the communication techniques. There are such agencies to be found in many aspects of marcom including PR, advertising, design, exhibitions, sales promotion and advertising.

They do offer focused expertise – but do not offer automatic integration since not all of the client's work is done in one place or even within one agency culture.

Bridging these two categories are market specialists. These are specialists in, for example, business-to-business or medical markets. They will offer something close to a one-stop shop within that limited field of operation.

At the other extreme from the first type mentioned above is what is often referred to as the 'boutique' approach. Here we find specialism within a very narrow field. Thus we find independent media planning and buying agencies and so-called 'creative hot shops' who develop the creative concept then hand it on for implementation.

It is virtually impossible to advise on the right approach to using agencies from this plethora of types without detailed knowledge of a given situation. The key is understanding the limitations of the in-house team. The guiding principle must be to seek to hire those who can best add value to your efforts at sensible cost.

GETTING THE BEST OUT OF AGENCIES

Simply, apply the three B's: briefing, bravery and budget!

The right brief

Nowhere is the old adage 'garbage in, garbage out' more true than in relationships with external agencies. Their members can be incredibly creative but they cannot read your mind or run your business. If you don't have a clear idea of what you want to achieve and the message you wish to put across, combined with a good understanding of your target audience, you give the agency little chance of producing effective communication.

Do your homework before calling in the agency. Brief them thoughtfully and clearly. Expect them to challenge the brief and to look for flaws in its logic. If they find any, eliminate them before proceeding.

Miss out any of these steps and it will be a miracle if you get the right campaign. It's more likely that you'll end up battling with the agency over the cost of arriving at a series of solutions which you have rejected. It will cost more than it needs to and you'll lose time on the project.

If the brief is right, it becomes easy to measure the proposals against a sensible yardstick; it meets the brief and delivers its message with impact, or it doesn't. That leads to getting the right communication out to the market, with the added bonus that rejecting work becomes a matter of rejecting a solution measured against its brief. That may sound curious, but creative people put real commitment into their work. They do not handle rejection easily. However, when a proposal can be shown to be off the brief, it is the proposal which is being turned down, not the individual who created it. This is a subtle but critically important point in building good, long-term agency relationships.

Committing to the solution

When you are presented with a solution which meets the brief, and has the added bonus of taking your breath away, buy it. Recognise that that initial reaction of yours is likely to be repeated among your target audience. You have found something with the impact to cut through the scream of competing communication out there in the media.

It does not matter that it isn't what you expected. It matters only that it fits the brand positioning, delivers the right message and has the emotional power to trigger a positive response among your audience. If it does, fight to protect its integrity against all of the would-be copywriters and designers within your company.

If you doubt the value of this approach, take a moment or two to think of the campaigns which stick in your own mind as a consumer. And recognise that the very best communication is communication which takes considered risks, which takes the brand on to new levels of perception in the eyes of its market.

Spend enough

I covered this point earlier in the planning process but it bears repetition. If the job is worth doing, it is worth doing well. If you can't afford to do it properly, then don't spend the money. Find another way to approach the problem, one which will get an effective result within the available funds.

And do tell the agency or agencies concerned what the budget is for each element, otherwise they're likely to waste time working on proposals which have no possibility of being accepted. Finally, allow the agencies to make a fair return on their efforts. An unprofitable agency is a poor long-term business partner – in both senses.

COMMUNICATE TO INTEGRATE

Another point worth a second airing: hold the communication together and ensure genuine integration. It is necessary to get all of those involved working well to the same brief.

Shared briefings are one route. Regular exchanges of views are essential. Get your partners together at least quarterly so they can update each other on their latest thinking and on progress on specific projects. Where you have briefed the lead technique before the others, have the lead agency present its proposals formally to the others. Make sure everyone understands the underlying strategy and the reason why the work looks and sounds as it does.

18

Internal Communication

What we do externally can be both of major interest and a valuable motivator within the organisation. We all like to see the reputation of our employer – and of its brands – rise in the public view. Conversely, we feel let down if our friends, or even worse a customer, is first to tell us about some new communication campaign being run by our colleagues. So there are both positive and defensive reasons for ensuring our staff are kept informed about what we are doing.

However, the overwhelming reason in many companies is much more fundamental: our people and their behaviour can have a significant influence on the perception of our brand.

As I write, Lynx, the parcel delivery service, is running a campaign based on the positioning 'we deliver reputations'. The proposition is that Lynx visits its customers' customers more than they do. Therefore every delivery Lynx makes can have an impact on the reputation of its customer. Imagine the response to such a campaign if every driver were surly and unhelpful, or administration staff were rude and uncaring in handling telephone queries. The positioning would be dead in the water.

This is by no means an isolated case. The service sector is a dominant part of many economies. Service depends heavily on the performance of people. Ultimately, they *are* the brand.

MERCHANDISE THE CAMPAIGNS

In recognising this, our first step must be to let people know what's happening, to keep them in the picture. That means creating the tools of communication at the same time as we develop the programme.

These do not need to be elaborate productions: a simple brochure showing ads and direct mail; a brief newsletter or even a memo giving sample press clippings on a regular basis; a few copies of an exhibition stand design put up on notice boards. Things like these are all that is needed to let staff see that we care about keeping them informed.

We could go a little further. Invest in framed proofs of a new advertising campaign and display them prominently around the sites. Put TV monitors into reception areas to run a loop of the latest commercials. Put staff on the mailing list for all new direct mail campaigns.

ENCOURAGE THE BRAND CULTURE

These tools are just the beginning. Our campaign proposition is based on a set of brand values. If our staff are important in substantiating those values, we need to nurture the culture – to monitor that our corporate, and therefore our individual behaviour is consistent with those values.

Those values must have been rooted in the existing behaviour in the first place – or we should have stopped the planning process and reviewed our direction. However, it is likely that the positioning is pushing those values further than their current state. That demands that we address our internal audience with all of the intellectual rigour we brought to bear on the external audiences.

We need to understand staff motivations in order to tap into them and show how our aspirations for the brand are consistent with their aspirations for themselves. We need to find the benefit proposition which will appeal to their self-interest and encourage them to behave in a manner which fully supports the brand positioning. We should be prepared to invest in research to pin that down in a meaningful way.

When we find an internal proposition and implement a staff communication programme based around it, we put in place the final piece of our jigsaw: we have truly integrated our marketing communication.

Further Reading

Some useful further reading is suggested below.

Brannan, T (1993) *The Effective Advertiser*, Butterworth-Heinemann.

Hart, N (1993) *Industrial Marketing Communications – Business-to-Business Advertising, Promotion and PR*, Kogan Page.

Kotler, P (1988) *Marketing Management – Analysis, Planning and Control*, Prentice-Hall.

Martin, D N (1989) *Romancing the Brand*, American Management Association, New York.

Morse, S (1994) *Successful Product Management*, Kogan Page.

Ogilvy, D (1985) *Ogilvy on Advertising*, Crown Publishers Inc., New York.

Smith, G (1994) *Getting the Best from Agencies*, Kogan Page.

Smith, P R (1993) *Marketing Communications – An Integrated Approach*, Kogan Page.

Stone, B (1984) *Successful Direct Marketing Methods*, Crain Books, Illinois.

Wilmhurst, J (1985) *The Fundamentals of Advertising*, Butterworth-Heinemann.

Wragg, D (1994) *The Effective Use of Sponsorship*, Kogan Page.

Yadin, D (1994) *Creating Effective Marketing Communications*, Kogan Page.

Index